W9-AAR-350

Zen Parenting

by Judith Costello and Jurgen Haver

Dedication

To Brian and Brenda Kilcup
who have always been there

And to Mary Costello
who is a *perfect* parent

We would like to thank the many people who helped bring this book into life. Most especially our thanks go to our agent Janet Rosen and the team at Sheree Bykofsky Associates, and to our wonderful editors at Robins Lane Press—Kathy Charner and Kate Kuhn—who took such care in going over each word. We are also deeply grateful to Robert Scott from Spirituality & Health *who took the time to not only review our manuscript but also to write a foreword. We want to thank all of our friends and family members who helped us greatly along the way, especially Jeanne Logsdon, Karen Easley, and John Young. We are also grateful to those who shared their parenting stories with us—especially Brian Biro and Mary Anne Thomas.*

zen
parenting

The Art of
Learning
What You
Already Know

Judith Costello
and Jurgen Haver

Robins Lane Press
a division of Gryphon House, Inc.
BELTSVILLE, MARYLAND

© 2004 Judith Costello and Jurgen Haver

Published by Robins Lane Press

10726 Tucker Street, Beltsville, MD 20705

800-638-0928 ✿ 301-595-9500 ✿ 301-595-0051 (fax)

Visit us on the web at www.robinslanepress.com

Library of Congress Cataloging-in-Publication Data

Costello, Judith, 1955-
  Zen parenting / by Judith Costello and Jurgen Haver.
    p. cm.
Includes bibliographical references.
  ISBN 1-58904-017-1
  1. Parenting–Religious aspects–Zen Buddhism. 2. Parent and child.
I. Haver, Jurgen, 1932- II. Title.
  HQ755.8.C675 2004
  649'.1–dc22

2003025956

Bulk purchase

Robins Lane Press books are available for special premium and sales promotions as well as for fund-raising use. Special editions or book excerpts also can be created to specification. For details, contact the Director of Marketing at the address above.

Disclaimer

The publisher and the authors cannot be held responsible for injury, mishap, or damages incurred during the use of or because of the information in this book. Every effort has been made to locate copyright and permission information.

table of contents

foreword

I once saw a cartoon depicting two meditators sitting cross-legged. One is answering a question his partner has just posed: "Nothing's next," he explains. "This is it."

In addition to being a wry insight into the challenge of mindfulness, the sketch tells us something important about being a parent, I believe. The birth of a child stuns us with the realization that our lives will never be the same. It enlivens us with the awareness that we've embarked on life's greatest adventure while assuming its most awesome responsibility. Every ounce of fear and every jolt of enthusiasm we experience are amply justified.

Yet, most of our moments as parents are not lived on heightened levels of suspense, joy, or transcendence. Instead, they are typically mundane, repetitive, and overwhelmingly messy. We gaze at the crying infant, the stubborn toddler, or the suddenly alien teenager and ask the same question as the meditation student in the cartoon: "So...what's next?"

And life gives us the answer: "This is it."

These thoughts came to me while reading Judith Costello and Jurgen Haver's gem of a book that you now hold in your hands. True to the "Zen" in *Zen Parenting*, they have built their engaging and practical compendium of stories, instruction, and exercises around the core concept of "accepting what is."

The book offers readers many gifts. First, there are the ones that I, in my judgmental and un-Zen fashion, think of as "happy." They allow us to experience fully those aspects of parenthood that might otherwise zip by us without notice. Through the concepts of "beginner's mind," paying attention, and not judging, Costello and Haver teach us to welcome

8 moments that a more anxious mindset might miss or dismiss while trying to wedge these genuine forces of nature—our children—into our narrow ideas of what they "ought" to be. The authors also lead us away from the "inadequacy trap" and show us how to go with—and appreciate—the flow. They even point the way toward sharing in the world of magic where our children live routinely.

This is not to say that a Zen parent inhabits an alternate universe where everything unfolds effortlessly and happiness reigns continuously. The book deals forthrightly with those less-than-happy moments when the squealing rubber meets the proverbial road by addressing the need to give discipline; the important differences among guilt, responsibility, shame, and blame; the value of work; and the challenges of divorce, illness, and dying. Wherever you are in your journey as a parent, the authors and the people whose stories they share have traveled that road and can serve as guides.

In fact, I've come to think of this book in terms of my own children's favorite game—the treasure hunt. The authors help us to discover the riches that are already strewn about the places we inhabit, but we don't see. As we unearth these treasures, we realize an even higher order of gifts. By shifting our perceptions and learning to work with "what is," we can become more aware and less anxious, more resourceful and less controlling. We can become people who are able to take what life hands us with equanimity and never lose touch with the love and the magic.

Wouldn't it be a wonderful gift to your children to let them grow up with such a parent? And wouldn't it be marvelous to have your children think of you as that kind of person? I know that's the gift I want, and so I treasure this book.

Robert Owens Scott
Editor in Chief, *Spirituality & Health* magazine
New York

introduction

Zen Parenting recognizes that in today's complex world there are no one-size-fits-all answers to parents' questions. Instead, this book proposes a way of living with children that is far better than a quick-fix formula. It is based on the undeniable truth that each child and each parent is unique. Rather than give ill-fitting advice, *Zen Parenting* offers insights on how parents can focus mindfully on daily experiences in order to transform the parent/child dynamic.

The concept of mindful awareness comes from Zen, a philosophy born in the East in a marriage of Buddhism and Taoism. It is a discipline that can aid parents in their roles as teachers, guides, and guardians of children. Whether the situation is a child with a "boo-boo," a grocery store tantrum, or a child's poor school work, if we, as parents, learn to pay close attention and release our judgments and expectations, we are practicing an ancient, incredibly useful precept—Zen mindfulness. And what does this careful attention do? It helps us tune in to the best, situation-specific response.

The automatic response to a child's tears might be just to hold the child. But there are times that call for a different response—and only mindful attention can tell us when those times occur. This book will help you tap into this kind of awareness.

Zen Parenting is based on complete attention to the beauty, the mystery, and the newness of each present moment. It offers a way to parent that is specific, appropriate, and less stressful than wearing the mantle of "perfect parent" expectations. It is a spiritual approach, a good-humored approach, and a forgiving approach. We believe it speaks directly to our modern world with an ancient wisdom.

Zen is a philosophy that enjoys the richness of paradox. That is why the subtitle of this book is a bit of a puzzle—if we already have the answers we need inside of us, why do we need to "learn what we already know?" The wisdom that we have within us at birth—a simple ability to pay attention and accept all of life—is like a buried treasure. It has been covered up by the weight of many, many experiences, which have led us to judge, expect, fear, and resent new encounters in life. For example, when a child has a tantrum in public, we tend to judge the child, expect him to behave differently, fear the judgments of others, and resent having to deal with the situation.

Yet, sometimes we are able to step past this mind clutter and discover an apparently simple solution. We know just exactly what to do. We respond appropriately and feel great about our abilities as parents. That is what tapping into "inner guidance" is all about. The answer isn't in a formula. It comes when we are paying close attention to the mystery at hand, in the same way a baby will pull apart a flower and then move on to the next one. It is a simple appreciation of life as it is.

One of the primary practices of Zen is to sit in meditation in order to stop the incessant thoughts and judgments of the mind. Eventually the practice of sitting in silence leads to some mind-expanding, "a-ha" insights. Does this mean that if you, as a busy parent, manage to make time to meditate then all problems will dissolve or all answers will come? Of course not. In fact, Zen masters insist that meditation should not be done with the expectation that "something will happen." The entire purpose of meditation is to be present in the moment—right here, right now. And that is much harder than it sounds.

Meditation, which attempts to still the racing-anticipating mind, is not a fast-food process. It is a discipline. It requires effort. What it does do, gradually and through regular practice, is to open up spaces in our lives, helping us to become free from the continual harassment of mind cluttering thoughts...Do this, do that, worry here, worry there, plan, be angry, be afraid, and on and on the thoughts go.

The silence of meditation prepares us to discover the endless riches in being aware of the here and now:

❀ the rich blue sky,
❀ the graceful gesture of a child pointing,
❀ the desperate need of a child screaming,
❀ the awesome gift of a teenager asking for help,
❀ and so much more, in our everyday, every-minute awareness.

Parents hear this phrase often—"Watch out. That child will grow up before you know it." The purpose of this book is to help you become a conscious parent, participating fully in every moment so that this warning won't come true. Because you will "know it!" You'll know the precious moments of being with your children.

11

12 Guidelines for Zen Parents

To the best of your ability live without expectation, anticipation, or regret. Learn to be present in the moment. There is a mystery to behold right now.

Accept what is happening now for what it is. This means be honest and non-judgmental. A Buddhist saying is, "Don't push the river." We are metaphorically trying to swim against the tide when we deny reality or expect things to be different than they are. Only by being honest are we prepared to act.

Take whatever action or non-action seems best in this very moment. That means make a conscious and considered decision about what needs to happen in this moment.

Let go of this moment because a new one is already here. Move away from spending too much time in hindsight. It detracts from being aware of the Now.

Surrender the Ego. Our desires to be seen and honored can get in the way of being able to teach and to listen. Great teachers know there is always more to know. We help our children best by being less self-conscious, and more honesty conscious.

Enjoy life's ironies. A famous Zen saying is, "Life is one continuous mistake." So much for striving for perfection! Life is a mistake when we focus on attaining the perfect body, the perfect family, the perfect life.

Pay attention to inner guidance. Wars have been fought over insisting that, "My way of life is the right way and you are wrong." The truth is there is only *one way*...but it is within each person and it is only found in stillness. It comes from paying attention to our deep inner urgings. And in following that inner guidance we do, in fact, join with all of life in the great Oneness of Being.

A Brief Summary of Zen Buddhism

Siddhartha was a prince who lived over 2500 years ago. He was eventually to become the Buddha, or the Enlightened One.

As a young man Siddhartha was deeply disturbed to learn that the world, outside his comfortable palace walls, was a place of illness, poverty, hardship and death. Wanting to better the lives of others, he set out to find an answer to the basic problem he saw in all of this—how to end suffering.

Siddhartha tried the life of a monk—renouncing everything— and yet this austerity only brought him close to death. After many years of wandering, he sat under a tree in meditation and vowed to remain there until he found the answer he sought. His Great Awakening happened when he realized these basic ideas: Life is filled with suffering and we must accept that "suffering is." The desire to avoid suffering is what keeps us trapped. When we release desires, resentments, anticipation, and fears, we are free to look for a solution to the problem at hand. We can end the torture of mind clutter—and thus end suffering—through mindful focus on the present moment and by learning to live "rightly." With this awareness Siddhartha became the Buddha.

Zen developed as Buddha's followers spread throughout Asia. Zen is a mixture of the Buddha's teachings with those of Taoism, which means "The Way." Zen focuses specifically on meditation (coming from Buddhism) and the search for balance in the midst of chaos (coming from Taoism). Zen comes from the word "zazen" meaning "to sit."

In *Zen Parenting* we refer to "accepting what is," which is a basic premise of Zen. This does not mean we should be passive or do nothing. Instead it means accepting reality without demanding that it be different than it is. What good are demands and wishes after all? They only confuse us and distract from the task at hand.

Does the Buddha's focus on acceptance of life mean, for example, we should peacefully accept abuse or violence in life? Absolutely not. What the Buddha realized is that denial of reality is a core reason people continue under oppression. When we accept the truth of our lives, then and only then, can we take the right action. The path to Enlightenment involves "right awareness, right concentration, right effort, and right action" (which are steps on the Eightfold Path of Buddhism). The purpose of this book is to help parents find these right ways of living even in the midst of childrearing challenges.

One of the Buddha's other bits of wisdom, which is also revealed in religions worldwide, is the realization that "this too shall pass." When problems arise we often feel overwhelmed and our whole world then becomes that problem. But the Buddha knew that life is an ebb and flow. A child having a tantrum does not define the child. "This too shall pass" is a special mantra for parents!

For more information on Buddhism see the Bibliography at the end of this book.

About "Living the Lessons"

In this book we use stories about adult experiences with children to illustrate Zen concepts. The use of stories, humor, and puzzles (called "koans") are traditional Zen methods for teaching. The anecdotes from our experience are followed by a reflection on the more universal meaning of these stories. At the end of each anecdote is an exercise—called "Living the Lesson"—that will help you apply the concepts of Zen to daily life. Regardless of what is written on paper, it is only when we commit to some action that we *own* the title of "Zen Parent."

The exercises in this book come out of Judith's work as an art therapist. In addition to the traditional Zen practice of meditation, this book includes exercises in painting, drawing, journaling, walking, reflecting, storytelling, and dreaming. All of these creative activities can be Zen experiences.

To be a Zen parent means to let go of rigid thoughts such as "I can't draw." Life is a grand adventure. It is in taking the leap of faith to try new things that we become "like the little children." And in such moments, we may very well say, "A-ha! This is what life is meant to be."

The magic of life flows from such willingness to *be like the child*.

beginner's mind:
today is everything

Chapter 1

*"And this our life...finds tongues in trees,
sermons in stones, and good in
everything."*
　　　—William Shakespeare, *As You Like It*

Beginner's mind is a Zen expression asking us
to look at everything as though for the very
first time. In other words, today's sunrise
doesn't compare with yesterday's. They are *not*
the same. Nothing is ever exactly the same. So,
see it afresh. For children, this perspective
comes easily—everything is exciting and new.
Each day is unique and special. Thus, children
live more fully in a state of beginner's mind.

For adults, however, this ability to enjoy the
newness in all things is obstructed because we
get caught up in mind clutter. We are easily
preoccupied. We are multi-tasking...doing the
laundry, while watching the kids, while
cooking the food, while answering the phone,
while planning tomorrow, while mulling over

18 conversations and problems, while wiping up spills. It's simply amazing how many directions we try to go in at the same time. Multi-tasking, although it appears to be required on occasion and was once touted as a new model for business, is actually less effective than doing things mindfully (total concentration on the project at hand). A lot of life's problems can be traced to these three things: we try to do everything at once, we become preoccupied with the past, and we anticipate the future. The truth is, the past is only a memory, it already happened. It is not real at this moment any more than the future is. The only place we can be alive is in this single precious moment. Our children need us to notice and be involved with them in the excitement of this moment—this *now*!

Being fully attentive to a child's "ow-ee" or his recitation of what happened at school—this is the first stage of beginner's mind. Focus on one thing at a time. Become filled with a sense of awe and appreciation. The child's wound needs our special gifts—the kiss that only we can give! The child's recitation is a fascinating look at a developing mind.

This chapter examines how to begin cultivating beginner's mind. First, plant your intention. Water it with daily focus. And let your children show you how to be awe-filled! To become a Zen parent, you must begin by focusing right here, right now.

Zen Points of Interest

In traveling across the western states there are road signs marking the way to spectacular views of jagged crevices and mountain skyscrapers—breathtaking panoramic views. So, when my family encountered those same "Point of Interest" signs while traveling through Kansas and Nebraska, we expected to be led to spots of awesome grandeur. The first such sign was in Nebraska. The land was flat in every direction. Cornfields and soybean plants dominated the landscape. After seeing a sign that said "Point of Interest ¼ mile" we began looking intently in all directions.

We asked the children and each other, "What special spot could possibly be here?" We saw a run-down wooden wagon resting on its rusted metal tongue. It pointed the way to a dirt path leading off into the horizon. In this midwestern flatland, the sky seemed to reach down and hold the earth.

However, we didn't find any panoramic views or spectacular cliffside drop-offs. We didn't spot even one "point of interest" that we thought was unique enough to warrant a sign. We laughed at our own expectations when we realized we had seen a most interesting rustic scene. There was beauty to be found everywhere and, without that sign to spark our curiosity, we might have failed to notice fields of sunflowers dancing across Kansas, or how the rich earth of the Midwest nurtures the prolific growth of plants, animals, and humans.

We decided a Zen master masquerading as a highway planner had erected the "Point of Interest" signs! He was reminding us that being alive means paying attention and honoring all that exists.

The Lesson

Parenting is an imperfect art similar to the road signs of that highway Zen master. The "Point of Interest"—the grand beauty—of the parenting process is sometimes very hard to see. Yet there is beauty in raising children, if we focus our awareness, if we sharpen our perceptions.

The Buddha, who lived over 2500 years ago, became aware that our struggle against reality is what leads us into suffering and unhappiness. He spoke about the sickness of the perceiving eyes—meaning we do not see all there is to see and the "not seeing" creates unhappiness.

To be a Zen parent means to just *be* with ourselves and with our ever-changing experiences. We do not need to talk about them, judge them, or analyze them. Instead, we can choose to simply accept what is. When we do this, all of life becomes a "Point of Interest." Everything shifts into newness. Everything awakens our sense of the mystery and reveals the miracle and grandeur of life, the gift of *now.*

Living the Lesson

Go for a "Zen walk" with your child. Identify the "points of interest"—you'll find them everywhere—in an oddly painted house, a gathering of storm clouds, a tiny flower pushing through the crab grass, and in the lines on an old woman's face. If you encounter things you would normally tend to judge, try to see them differently. See everything as a point of interest. When you return home spend 15 minutes journaling about what you have seen. Ask your child to draw pictures of what he or she discovered.

Zen Experts Are Inside

"Do not seek to follow in the footsteps of the wise. Seek what they sought."

– Matsuo Basho, 17th-century Japanese haiku poet

A woman in the checkout line at the library was carrying a stack of parenting books. She sighed. I asked her if the parenting books were helping. She laughed with resignation. "No. Most of the books on parenting don't help much. I keep checking out new ones in the hope that one of them will be of real help. As you can see, my son is challenging."

I looked over at her six-year-old son who had strewn several books on the floor. His mother stopped talking to me and told him to pick out the books he wanted and return the rest to the shelves. He ignored her. His mother turned back to me. "Nothing works. These books have lots of advice but none of it seems to apply to him or to me. Sometimes I think I should just follow my instincts."

We were both quiet for a few minutes. I closed my eyes trying to imagine us—two mothers—surrounded by a light. When I looked up the woman was calling to her

21

son, "Derrick, I'm checking out. If you don't give me the books you want now, you can't check out any of them." Suddenly, Derrick was motivated. He picked five books off the floor and brought them to his mother. She said, "I am only checking out these for you if you put all of the others back." Although Derrick pouted, he walked back to the books and put them back on the shelf. The mother smiled at me. Then she put her stack of parenting books in the return pile and checked out the five her son had picked for himself.

The Lesson

Parenting is an amazingly complex task—caring for the physical, emotional, educational, social, and spiritual needs of the young—yet people have been doing it for thousands of years. However awkwardly they have done it, it is only in the last half century that parents have felt they must rely on experts. Before that, parents simply didn't expect to do a perfect job. They took it one day at a time.

Certainly there are books that can offer helpful insights and provide suggestions that may be useful. However, the Buddha said that language cannot transfer wisdom; there is a limit to what can be taught with words. In truth, there is no manual that can show parents how to raise children.

It's not that the experts have *nothing* to offer, but too many modern parents have suppressed their own "inner expert." Parents need to trust themselves and listen to the help that comes from a regular practice of deep reflection and silent surrender to the immediate experience. We need to give up the expectation of perfection. Our children may suffer from the mistakes we make but they (and we) will also learn from them. The answers we seek can be found inside of each of us. When we let go of expectations and participate in life with full awareness, parenting will begin to flow—like a leaf floating on the river. Then we can flow with life and react to the present moment with complete abandon. How simple. How clearly appropriate.

Living the Lesson

Too often, we look for answers outside of ourselves because we have recurring thoughts of inadequacy. Watch your mind for those times when you are focusing on feelings of helplessness, inadequacy, or frustration. Whenever such feelings come up, challenge yourself with the following questions:

- ❀ Is my child growing?
- ❀ Am I taking care of him or her?
- ❀ Do I have to be perfect to be a parent?
- ❀ Do I expect perfection from my child?

After challenging negative thought patterns with questions like these, practice letting go and re-focusing. Turn your total attention to one object right in front of you. See it fully. See its shape, color, and patterns. Watch the play of light upon it. Experience it as fully as possible.

Zen From the Mouths of Babes

(Contributed by Brian Biro, author of *Beyond Success.*
Reprinted from *Upline* magazine with permission.)

*Several years ago, when we lived in the Bitterroot Valley
in Montana, my wife, Carole and my two children,
Kelsey and Jenna, went out one evening to our favorite
café in our town of Hamilton. The café was located on
the second floor of an old brick Main Street building and
served delicious meals in a comfortable and casual
atmosphere. As we made our way to our table, we were
hardly noticed. The other diners were involved in their
own separate worlds, scanning the menu, eating quietly,
or softly conversing.*

*The café's walls were huge panoramic windows that
opened to view magnificent mountains on both sides of
the valley. Literally five miles from where we sat, the
Bitterroot Mountains exploded up from the valley floor,
rising over 10,000 feet. On the opposite side stood the
almost florescent Sapphire Mountains, more gentle as
they sloped gradually to heights of 7,000 and 8,000 feet,
yet almost mystical in the way light played along the
ridges, seeming to glow from inside the rock. But, as we
sat down and established our own little "turf" at our
table, we saw only our menus and our trials and
tribulations from the day.*

*After a moment or two, Jenna, four years old at the time,
stood up and walked over to the huge windows. We didn't
even notice her until suddenly the polite quiet of the café
was shattered with an exuberant shout of exaltation
from our little girl. As she looked out the window, a light
of awareness so real, so exciting, and so present had*

*flashed into her spirit. She whirled around and shouted
at the top of her lungs as she pointed out the window,
"Look Mommy, Daddy, Kelsey—we're in heaven!"
Instantly the entire café became completely silent. Then,
after a moment, as Jenna's exclamation settled into our
collective consciousness, I watched a magical
transformation take place. Smiles swept through the café,
and people began talking with joy and animation, not
just with their own parties, but also across the invisible
barriers between tables. It suddenly felt like a big family,
sharing, laughing, and connecting.*

*When my face returned to its normal color after my
initial embarrassment, I began to see a beautiful truth.
My four-year-old daughter was brilliant. She alone saw
heaven where the rest of us saw our tables. She saw
beauty, possibility, and wonder where all we saw were
menus and invisible barriers. Her radiant breakthrough
woke us up and inspired us to see with new eyes and
created an entirely new experience.*

The Lesson

Children can be our teachers if we will let them. Our children
are usually more readily focused in the present moment than
we adults are. As a result, they experience the inherent magic
of the everyday world. When we join them in their perspective
they will often share the kind of magic Jenna saw.

Adults lose the natural ability to be present in the "now" by
trying to categorize reality. It is, in part, a linguistic problem. As
we grow, we learn symbols to describe things. The word
"mountain" conveys an image and yet it cannot capture the
unique colors, shape, or feeling of any specific mountain…it's
never the "real thing." The word "mountain" and our

25

interpretation of it remove us from experiencing the real thing. Thus, we can be in a beautiful setting and not connect with it. We have our "adult perspective"—this is simply a café in the mountains—nothing more.

We often do the same symbol stereotyping of our children. We have a mental picture of who "Sarah" is so we stop seeing the real child. We relate to the label of "sweet Sarah" or "ADHD Sarah" instead of the ever-changing child who lives with us. We expect her to like milk because she liked it yesterday—and we're unhappy if she doesn't like it today. We don't really want Sarah to change.

It takes practice to focus on the present and to let go of our symbolic thinking. But we did it once, when we were children. It's time to return to seeing with the eyes of a child.

Living the Lesson

Look out the window closest to you. Imagine you are four years old. How would you interpret this view? Is there any magic here? Draw a picture of what you see and give it to your child. It doesn't matter if you think you can draw. When you were four you didn't think about whether or not you could draw. You didn't even know what a "masterpiece" was and couldn't have cared less. You just drew. For children, and for adults who are willing to suspend judgment, drawing and painting are powerful tools for focusing and re-focusing energy. They help us focus on the experience of seeing.

Zen Means Accepting What Is...

Monica was a young mother who cleaned houses to support her family. For six dollars an hour she went to other people's houses with a playpen, two small children, and cleaning supplies in tow.

Monica would pull a bulky playpen out of her car while holding a baby on her hip. She carried both inside while instructing her three-year-old son to stay close by. Within minutes of entering the house, Monica had the playpen set up, with her young son and baby comfortably inside. She sang to her children while she scrubbed floors and dusted. When her older child begged to get out, she complied—sending him on errands around the house as her baby slept.

I asked her how she managed it all. Imagining myself in her shoes, I knew I might feel resentful. How could she be paid so little for so much work? How would she manage when the children were older and more active? And why are those darn playpens so totally un-portable? But Monica didn't concern herself with any of these questions. Smiling, she said to me, "This is my life. I take it one day at a time."

The Lesson

The truth of Zen practice is this—life happens. We don't control things or other people. The place where we have power, and where our thoughts determine our reality, is in how we interpret and integrate the realities of life. Our attitude toward the world determines our experience of it.

27

28 Monica chose not to resent the job or the children or the playpen. Her life is "what is." Until she found new options for employment, she chose to accept her life and to enjoy it. Was this simple-minded or just simplifying? I believe she knew how to let go of expectations, wishes, and imaginings in order to enjoy the little miracles of each day. She gave her complete attention to the immediate moment.

Living the Lesson

Imagine you wake up one morning and your child is sick, the heater is no longer heating, and the car won't start. Your house is cold. Your child is shivering and it is too early to call a doctor or a repair person. Is it a horrible day?

Is it possible that this could be an opportunity? You and the children need to huddle together for warmth. Tickling helps pass the time. The child who is coughing can be wrapped in blankets and snuggled in your arms. This is a time for stories, for laughter, for doing things differently. Ask yourself, What is the "adventure" in this day?

Now let go of all the images and focus on breathing. Breathe in. Breathe out. Feel the warmth of the breath. Feel its life-giving freshness. All there is—is breath. Focus right here, right now on breathing.

the
inadequacy
trap

Inadequacy. It's one of the biggest obstacles to becoming a better parent. Yet it comes unbidden in response to the newness of the job. There's so much to learn and so little time to take it all in; it can feel overwhelming. And it's clear that parents are faced with more choices and decisions than ever before about:

- ❀ schools (home school, public school, private school, or a new alternative),
- ❀ medical care (traditional, homeopathic, naturopathic, etc.)
- ❀ diet (traditional meal plans vs. a vegetarian diet; organic, natural food; or other special diet)
- ❀ socializing and safety (playgroups, child care, neighbors, unsupervised play in the yard, or supervised play at the park)
- ❀ discipline (family conferences, 1-2-3 time out, let the child decide vs. parental authority...lots of conflicting advice)

30   The choices, possibilities, information, and advice seem without end.

And, the relationship between us as parents with our particular children is an all-new, never-before-experienced occurrence. There is no blueprint, no one-size-fits-all formula. We are on our own to make all these decisions.

Without mindfulness, we might sink into feelings of inadequacy. When the feeling of inadequacy is not observed and released—the "monkey mind," an ever-busy trickster, will try to cope by:

- ✿ blaming someone else
- ✿ playing the "one-up-manship game"—"At least my child is better than _____."
- ✿ feeling the "poor me" woes

All these are attempts by the mind to ignore the pain of inadequacy. It takes effort and awareness to keep from trying to blame someone or something for today's confusion and mistakes. But with mindful attention we can see there is no one to blame.

Did our parents, or our spouse, or outside influences, or our less-than-perfect response contribute to our child's behavior? Possibly. But is blaming ourselves or someone else helpful? No. Blame, in all its forms, is unhealthy and can become an excuse for doing nothing to improve the situation.

Let's face it. Before we had a child we probably had no idea how challenging it was going to be. The only way to cope is one day at a time, one minute at a time—apologizing for wrongs, and taking action to make things better.

Responsible action is the only useful antidote to problems. A Zen perspective can help us detach from the blame-and-shame game so that we become more responsive to each moment as it arrives.

Letting Go of Anticipation

When my friend suggested we go for coffee and that I should bring Brigit, my busy three-year-old, I was nervous. Mary was suggesting a new and popular bakery—an adult hangout. I didn't want to disturb the other patrons or face the judgment or annoyance of others if my daughter didn't behave. But Mary and I needed to talk. So off we went.

At the bakery, Brigit asked if she could "read the papers" (the free ones by the door). I told her she could get one and then come and sit at the end of our table. As she wandered off between tables my eyes stayed on her. I was ready to jump up and retrieve her should another customer act irritated.

A dark-haired woman sat down at a nearby table. She had a book with her and her glasses rested low on her nose, ready for a quiet interlude. Brigit had retrieved her newspaper and was on her way back when the dark-haired woman caught her attention. "What are you eating?" Brigit asked.

The woman looked at Brigit in surprise. I cringed. My muscles tensed to leap forward. But to my surprise the woman began talking to my daughter. Brigit pulled herself into a chair next to the woman and stayed there

31

for 20 minutes. For most of that time I remained on edge…I was sure that the woman would find it tiresome to talk to my daughter. I could imagine Brigit going on and on talking about food, her brother, and a story she was making up. She was in a very talkative stage.

The woman nodded occasionally and ate her food.

As the woman got ready to leave, she walked Brigit back to our table. She introduced herself and said, "Today is my birthday, and I wanted to treat myself to a special lunch. I thought I would have a quiet meal and do some reading. But your daughter was the real birthday treat for me. I haven't enjoyed myself this much in a long time."

We hugged—a mom, a stranger, and a little girl enjoying an unexpected bond.

The Lesson

It is always a surprise to me how frequently and easily we are distracted from the experience of today by our anticipation and expectations. When it comes to our children, we are full of both. We want the best for them but we are so afraid things won't work out. We anticipate the child's failing or other people's condemnations. When we can release these two things we have the chance to experience the beauty of our children.

Today is not something that can be predicted. That is perhaps the hardest lesson of life. We want to know what will happen and control the outcome. Yet when we can let go, reality often far exceeds our expectations. The world is full of mystery and possibility. If we can just wait for it to unfold, the surprises will astound us.

That is what happened on this day at the bakery. I expected the worst—that my daughter would be unwanted and out of place. But I was blessed with a beautiful lesson: my daughter had great gifts to share and she blessed the life of a stranger. And, she changed the world, for just a few moments, with her little-girlness.

Living the Lesson

Plan to take two walks today, one in the morning and one in the evening. On the first walk look for three things: a red rock, a green leaf, and a white feather. Are you able to find these things? How does it feel to be focused in this way?

During the evening, take another walk. This time surrender all expectations. Focus on nothing in particular. Allow yourself simply to be in your body and outdoors. Feel the air, the wind, and the rocks underfoot. Smell the trees and night air. Observe and feel it all.

Afterwards reflect on the difference between the two walks. How did it feel to let go? Did you see more or less on the second walk? Do this with your children. Show them the value of being open to the experience without expectation.

The Inadequacy Trap

34 The Zen Master

(From *Zen Miracles* by Brenda Shoshanna, copyright © 2002 Brenda Shoshanna. Reprinted by permission of John Wiley & Sons, Inc.)

There is a wonderful story about a great Zen Master who was called by his brother and asked to come home and help with his nephew. The boy had become a rebel, staying out late at night, smoking, drinking, and making trouble. No matter how hard others tried to change and help him, he would listen to no one. His behavior grew worse daily, and the family was frightened.

The Zen Master agreed to visit for one week. He arrived at his brother's home and just went along with the daily routine, speaking pleasantly to the nephew about this and that, never mentioning his behavior. The nephew kept waiting for his uncle to reprimand him. Instead, the Master accompanied his nephew on his trips here and there. They spent time together, and still the Master said nothing.

Finally, the week passed and the time came for the Master to go home. The nephew stood close by, waiting for the scolding. Instead, as the Master bent over to tie his shoes, he began to cry silently. The nephew saw teardrops rolling down the Master's cheeks and was deeply shaken. He could not move or say a word. From that time on, his behavior changed. He could not act the old way, even if he wanted to.

The Lesson

The Zen Master knew this boy didn't need more judgment and criticism. Love made the difference. Without words, the Master communicated both his complete love for the boy and his great sadness that the boy was making choices that could lead to serious harm. And this caring created a miracle of transformation in the boy.

Should his parents have done what the Zen Master did in the first place? Probably not. It was their responsibility as parents to point out to the boy that his behavior was unacceptable and needed to change.

Judgment is not the same as discernment. To judge the boy's behavior wouldn't help the situation. But to assess the situation honestly and truthfully, a parent would have to say, "This behavior will lead to self destruction if it is not interrupted."

The question is, how do we help a child who is traveling down an unhealthy path? Will it help to review why he has come to such behavior? That is the therapy approach—to understand what went wrong in this parent/child/life dynamic. But the child was in more immediate need. And whatever the historical reasons were, these parents had a child headed for trouble. They needed to say, "This is unacceptable. This behavior has to stop."

One of the lessons of this story is that sometimes parents need to call for help from an outside mentor—some other adult the child respects and may be able to talk to. Parents don't need to do it all. Children thrive best when they have many adults to relate to.

36   The other lesson of this story is that love can heal and words can hurt. The parents expected the Zen Master to talk to the boy. Instead, he communicated without words. Much can be said by our actions.

Living the Lesson

Be open to your children's friends. Let them and their parents know you care. In this way, you build community. Use this art exercise as a reflection on the many experiences and influences that will have an impact on your child.

Try this: Fold a piece of construction paper in half and make cuts up from the fold edge to 1" from the other edge. Make parallel cuts 1" apart. (See drawing.) Use odd fabric scraps from your child's old clothes or from the household to create a weaving in this "loom."

 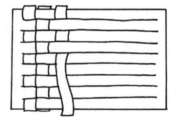

Use pieces that are 10" x 1". Weave these strips of fabric in and out of your loom. Over and under, in and out. Imagine this is your child. The fabric pieces represent the people and experiences in your child's life. Somehow, this hodge-podge of influences helps create the adult your child will become. Some of these influences are under your control. Others are beyond your control. Such is the tapestry of life.

Zen and Self-Condemnation

The woman was feeling guilty and responsible for this situation—the two-year-old had problems with his teeth. "Bottle mouth," the dentist said. The woman felt engulfed in shame. Yet, she had done what she felt was right. Her little boy had been sickly as a baby and needed comfort. She couldn't nurse him because she had also been very sick. She had complied with his requests for a bottle, weaning him just a few weeks before he turned two.

Another dentist explained it differently, "It is partly genetics, partly the chemistry of the child's mouth, partly the bottle, partly the care of these early teeth. And really the issue is—the teeth don't look good now. We go from today."

The mom had trouble letting go and moving forward. But she knew the shame she felt was unproductive. That afternoon as she left the dentist's office with her husband and their little boy, she said, "I'm sorry I let him have the bottle that long. I did what I thought was best at the time. Let's move forward and do the right thing now."

The Lesson

Guilt is a reminder from our inner self when we commit a wrong action. It is there to say, "Be responsible."

Responsibility means owning the mistake and righting the problem.

Shame is a reaction to wrongdoing. Like guilt, it can be used to call us to be accountable.

37

38   *Blame* is when we try to make someone else responsible for our wrongdoing. It is looking for fault in someone else.

When children are punished because they make a *mistake*, for which they already feel guilty, they learn that they are not allowed to make mistakes. And, feeling incapable of achieving perfection, they may opt for total "imperfection." The answer to this is to understand that mistakes happen. And the appropriate response to mistakes is to change what can be changed.

Milk is spilt. Father and child work together to make sure it gets cleaned up. Maybe there is even time for a bit of laughter in the process, or a memory of times when father spilt the milk and how Grandma responded. The way to teach healthy responsibility is to let the child own up to what he or she actually did.

To be responsible means to say, "I did this. I made a mistake. I was thoughtless. I will correct the situation by cleaning up the spilt milk."

Living the Lesson

Make a "Mistake/Responsibility Jar." In this jar, put small notes about mistakes you have made recently. The purpose of this is to acknowledge them and to learn not to carry them around like placards saying, "Hit me. I made a mistake."

Make sure you have done what you could to rectify each situation. Then realize you put the mistake and the action taken into the jar. Release it. Don't carry it with you.

After there are a few notes in the jar, make a ritual of burning them. Go outside with the jar. Place the notes in an iron pot and put a match to them. This is a symbol of turning them over to the universe. Put in some dried plants as well. This is a symbol of healing. Once the notes are burned, they are gone. Let the mistakes go. Teach your children to also accept responsibility for mistakes, to take action and then to release the burden of guilt.

Notes to ponder: Blame is to accuse, point a finger, find fault. Responsibility is to accept that every action sets a series of events into motion, and that the initial action is the generating factor. This is learned behavior. Children do not think that to turn the hose on outside and then forget about it means a lot of water is wasted and something may be flooded. They do not possess a natural understanding of cause and effect. Parents need to teach this. And it takes great patience to teach children about consequences. They usually need many lessons.

The Inadequacy Trap

humor transforms

"Humor tells us that the mind works in patterns but that it is possible to switch the patterns."

—Edward de Bono,
Handbook for the Positive Revolution

More than any other Buddhist school, Zen encourages the use of humor to teach, promote understanding, and jar awareness. This is because humor forces a change of perspective. It also frees us to enjoy ourselves. Because life is such an unknown, winding path, it is best to enjoy the journey and not focus on the destination. We're sure to become "lost" many times. Humor allows us to re-frame any experience into an adventure. In doing so, we find our way again.

Humor has many benefits. Recent studies and brain research suggest that humor increases our creative thinking potential. (For more information on the benefits of humor, see page 144 for the website of Edward de Bono.) It helps you to release worries. As the old adage goes, "Worry is interest paid on trouble before

42   it is due." The best way to face adversity of any kind is to find a little humor in the situation. It's not by accident that so many comedians use their own lives as material. Life is funny if you choose to see it that way.

The Zen Dinner

We had set aside an evening to go out to dinner. Our reservations were made and everything was readied for a romantic evening by ourselves. However, through a series of unfortunate events, both children ended up coming along with us on our date.

The children became noisy and demanding as soon as we entered the restaurant. Thankfully, our server was excellent. She brought a basket of crayons, sheets of paper, and two books to read. We each took a book and began to read to the children. The rest of the diners uttered a collective sigh of relief. Of course, this was a short-lived respite. In a few moments the room was once again entertained by our loud conversation: "Where's the food?" and "Why can't we leave?" and "I have to go potty!"

After eating a few bites of food and distracting them as much as possible so that we could have a little bit of conversation, we left the restaurant. Driving away, Judith took my hand and said with a laugh, "That was nice, honey. It's been so long since we've had a romantic dinner—just the two of us."

The Lesson

This story involves several decision points. We could have chosen to be upset with the sitter. How dare she cancel at the last minute! We could have chosen to be angry with the children. How dare they ruin our night! Or, we could have taken the children home feeling absolute resentment. Instead, the wisdom of our Zen practice led us to believe the children and the babysitter couldn't ruin our night unless we let that happen. We chose to let the children and the sitter off the hook by bringing the children along on our date.

The evening turned out to be an opportunity to practice observing our choices and ourselves. That is a Zen practice: Pay attention. Let the feelings pass. Use humor to turn the instant perception around.

However, parents do have a responsibility to not let their children ruin other people's evenings. On this occasion, there were quiet periods of cooperation in between the more difficult times. To be a Zen parent in such circumstances requires flexibility. Many parents of young children opt to avoid fine-dining establishments as a family. It is easier to go to "kid-friendly" (albeit "adult-unfriendly") establishments. Although such places are entertaining for the children, the food is unhealthy. As a budding Zen parent, try making it a rule to skip fast-food restaurants and go to places where the atmosphere and food is good for all.

A Zen parent isn't perfect. But a Zen parent takes a moment to practice paying attention before responding to a new situation. A Zen parent knows that:

- ❀ Life rarely unfolds the way we wish it would. Demanding that life conform to our expectations only sets us up for failure.
- ❀ The initial feelings of embarrassment will pass as we pay attention to the children and ourselves.

43

✿ We can respond with humor and re-direction rather than confrontation. These are skills any parent can learn with practice.

✿ Children rise to the occasions we offer to them. Without punishing them or shaming them, our children can learn to behave appropriately in public.

✿ Perfection is impossible. Although we would all like our children to be perfect and our responses to them to be perfect, we know that is not realistic. We can only do our best and keep paying attention!

Living the Lesson

When you wake up in the morning, look in the mirror. Observe your wild hair, the slight (or not-so-slight) bags under your eyes, and the imprint of the pillow on your skin. Then laugh. Make your hair even messier. Make a funny face. Don't take yourself seriously. Teach your children to begin the day this way, too.

Zen Raspberries

Peter picked raspberries with his kindergarten class but didn't want to eat them.

"If we eat them, they'll be all gone!" he complained.

I said, "If we don't eat them they'll go bad instead."

Peter continued to worry about losing his treasure. So, we changed our strategy. Jurgen said, "Those raspberries have already gone bad."

Peter and I looked at him in disbelief.

"Yep. I caught them fighting with the olives this morning and they were pushing the grapes out the refrigerator door. Did you know the raisins have declared war on those raspberries? It's definitely time for them to go!"

Peter looked surprised—then he laughed as he opened the refrigerator. We had a feast of raspberries that very afternoon.

The Lesson

Most of us have trouble living in the moment. Like Peter, we want to hold on to what we have; yet in holding on, what we love slips away. A key Zen perspective is to let go. Embrace what *is*. The only reality is what is here now. Clinging doesn't keep it here—it just makes it "go bad."

Peter's raspberries were fresh from the vine, filled with flavor. Yet, if the berries weren't eaten, they would wither into bitterness. Humor is a tool we can use to help children let go. It works effectively for children beginning around the age of four. Humor, when it is not a put-down, can help children push past those things that hold them back. Humor is the only thing that helped Peter move away from dwelling on the negative possibilities. Now he knows that raspberries can be "bad!" On a subconscious level he also knows that life moves forever forward. There is no looking back.

46   Humor heals. It helps all of us to see life from a fresh
perspective, and jars us out of our pre-set ideas. When we feel
mired in wanting to keep things the same although they are
changing, we can picture the raspberries jumping out of their
bowl to go hit the olives. The bulbous berries are scowling
while the olives hold up their pimentos in fear! The olives are
yelling, "Somebody! Please eat those raspberries!"

Living the Lesson

Imagine how you might transform your child's fears with
humor. For the child who is afraid of the dark, practice making
faces and scary sounds to scare the dark away! In this way you
help your child take control of the dark and scary world, and
your child will see that it doesn't seem so dark anymore!

Zen on a Heavy Day

*Once, when my day had not gone well, I snapped at the
children. It created instant tension in the house. Brigit
was on the verge of tears. Peter went to the kitchen table
pouting. I realized I had to do something, and so I
reinterpreted my "bad" day for them. I said, "I didn't
mean to yell at you, but I had a really heavy day
today...I think it weighed a thousand pounds! I couldn't
carry it so I gave it to Joe. But, you know him; he passed
it off to Bob. Bob gave it right back to me! But now
you're home and I thought I'd pass it off to you. But you
look squashed. So I'm dropping it. How's that?!"*

I scraped the imaginary load off the children's backs and let it drop to the floor with a verbal "THUD."

The Lesson

It is important to own up to our mistakes. But confessing doesn't have to be a serious experience! Children are always ready to forgive, especially when we transform the experience into something fun.

Living the Lesson

Think about the last three mistakes you've made. Did you bark at your husband or wife? It may have been a metaphorical barking, but apologize by literally barking! Did you forget to take your son to the game? Apologize by telling him you lost your brain. "Sweetie, have you seen it? It's been missing for days!"

Laugh at yourself and others will laugh too. Like everything else in life, learning the art of humor takes practice. With time, you'll get better and better. It's worth it, too, because this is one of Zen's most powerful tools. Sharpen it every day and your house will become a fun place to live in.

Try a family belly laugh. Each member of the family lies on the floor, resting their heads on another person's belly. Then one person begins by saying, "Ha-ha-ha." This makes their head move a bit. The person they are resting on is likely to begin a more real "ha-ha." And the laugh will spread until the heads are bouncing!

Humor Transforms

"No, I Won't Get Dressed!"

When I told my five-year-old, "Get dressed right away, we're late for school," he responded with a resounding, "No!" In the past this would lead to an argument, a test of wills. But I tried to see his response as a request to play. I responded. Play for play.

"I wonder if you can get dressed before I count to 100. One, two, three . . . "

Result? We set a new getting-dressed record at our house, down from 20 minutes of arguing and complaining to four fast-flying minutes of laughing and having fun. What happened? I had accidentally moved from my world of "do-it-because-it's-time-to-do-it" to his world of "life-is-a-game-and-is-supposed-to-be-fun."

Next came the challenge of getting my three-year-old dressed. With her, the resistance was a bit different. She pretended she couldn't hear. Being ignored is really irritating, but I have learned that humor and redirection are more fun than fighting and usually open the door for change. I pretended I didn't know I was being ignored and began pulling out clothes for her. "This one is pretty but I really like the blue in this top. What do you think?" She still ignored me.

Now, one parenting model might be to figure out what she was trying to avoid and try talking her through the resistance. But I thought her resistance was rooted in testing the limits.

So I tried a different tactic. I said, "What do you think?

How does this look on me?" I put one arm through her shirt and hung the rest of it on my head. She laughed wildly.

"That doesn't fit you!" she said.

"Oh, it doesn't? I really like it. Don't you think it makes me look younger and smarter?" I replied.

She, of course, claimed the outfit and took it away from me. But that still didn't mean she put it on. It only meant she was in a good mood. We both had a twinkle in our eyes by then. I said, "Okay, if I give you this shirt, you have to put it on to see if it really fits you. Because I think it fits me better."

That was enough play to set the stage for her to get dressed. But, of course, every morning is different. There is no formula. However, being willing to engage children where they live—in the land of play and imagination— usually prepares them to cooperate with you.

The Lesson

So what is really happening during these morning spats of resistance?

I think the children simply need to know they can say "no." After all, they aren't the ones who have to get to work. They have other priorities. Once they are aware they have the freedom to say "no," they usually become more than willing to help out. The lesson for us is to recognize the children as autonomous beings with minds and wills of their own. The first time I gave my child the freedom to say "no," I felt a great exhilaration by his sudden willingness to do what I asked.

49

A lot of this has to do with respect. It is very frustrating to feel you have no choices. If you want to remember what it feels like, observe two children from the same family. One is two and the other is five. Ask the two-year-old a question. Does the two-year-old get to answer you? Most likely, the five-year-old will pop up with the answer. See the disappointment on the two-year-old's face. That scene is a cameo of what the parent-child relationship can turn into if you're not careful.

Living the Lesson

Practice "magic" with your child. Make magic wands out of sticks, ribbons, and jewels. (See the illustration.) Then, when there is a lack of cooperation try waving the wand over the child. "Abracadabra, you are dressed now!" If this doesn't work, hold the child's clothes in your hand and wave the wand. As you finish a long "Abracadabra," stick the wand through the shirt sleeve and say, "Oops, it's going on the wrong thing." Have fun. Laugh together. See what a little magic can do for you.

balancing the
opposites

Chapter 4

"All nature is but art unknown to thee,
All chance, direction thou canst not see;
All discord, harmony not understood...
One truth is clear, whatever is, is right."
—Alexander Pope, *An Essay on Man* (0383)-21

Taoism and Buddhism met, and from the two, Zen was born as the ever-questioning, often laughing, sometimes irreverent offspring!

In the Tao, meaning "The Way," we learn that things that appear as opposites are actually one. Male and female, yin and yang, form a balanced whole. The universe is One and nothing can be divided and separated without losing the sense of the whole. In understanding this, we find relief from the need to pick sides and to condemn differences.

Lao Tzu, author of the *Tao Te Ching*, described "The Way" as being able to see simplicity within that which seems complicated. He reminds us to find greatness in little things.

Strength in weakness. Commonalties within differences. These are lessons our children already know and can teach us. Young children often prefer pots and pans to bang on rather than fancy electronic toys. They can see beauty in a tiny weed. They don't care if the person they are with is big or small, old or young—the only requirement is "Will they play?" It is the process of growing and "socializing" that causes children to forget these simple insights. They become distracted just as adults do, and then weeds become a bother and pans become useful only for cooking.

There are some specific sets of "opposites" pertaining to the life of parents. When these opposites are reconciled, children can be appreciated and better understood. When understood, the clamoring of the opposites can be seen as an attempt at wholeness.

The following opposites are necessary to make a whole:

- ✿ Continuity and Change
- ✿ Empty and Full
- ✿ Ordinary and Extraordinary

The word "Zen" comes from "zazen," meaning "to sit." We invite you to sit with the apparent opposites until they become for you a Oneness.

Zen Attention: Continuity vs. Change

Janice liked to put her daughter's hair in pigtails. It was their morning ritual and it was always the same. Then, one day, her daughter said, "Mom, I'm getting too old for pigtails. Would you braid it, please?"

Janice looked down and saw her daughter for the first time in months. She was growing and she had changed. As she braided her daughter's hair, she thought, "How did this happen without my noticing? She is growing up and I'm missing it."

The Lesson

Adults respond to many things out of habit, believing this is the way things are. How many times does someone ask us something that we should know, and we can't remember because we haven't really thought about it for so long? The same thing happens with our children. We assume we know what is going on inside each of them, without really thinking about it. But children change, just as we change, from moment to moment. If we expect the children to stay the same, we will miss out on the mystery of who they are each day. The only way to keep up with the changes is to make certain we keep coming back to the moment.

How many times do we hear parents say, "They grow up too fast!" Imagine each day as a new beginning and take mental note of the wonder-filled changes all around. Who are these beings you live with? How do they talk? What are they trying to say? What do they need from you?

We have the opportunity to make *paying attention to our priorities* a constant point in the ever-changing flux of life.

53

54 Living the Lesson

One man who heads a major music studio shared what he considers to be the secret of his success: "Every day I sit quietly and still my mind. Then after the mind chatter has stopped, I ask myself three questions:

- ✿ What do I need to do for my children and wife today? (my duty)
- ✿ What do I need to do for myself today? (my sustenance)
- ✿ What do I need to do to make the world better today? (my service)

I let each question settle in. And clear messages always come to me."

Try this man's secret for success. Close your eyes. Relax. Breathe. Use your breathing as a focusing tool. When your mind has become still, ask yourself those three questions.

Zen Fullness: Empty vs. Full

Jamie and Terry worked furiously, digging in the field. Each tried to be the one who could remove the most dirt. Jamie beheld the growing mountain of dirt. It was almost as tall as he was. In his eyes he saw a backyard Mt. Everest. "This will be great," he said. "We can slide down it, and once we pack it hard we can ride our bikes up it." Jamie's eyes gleamed in delight as he imagined the neighborhood kids wanting to climb up the hill. And he would be in charge. He imagined himself saying, "It's my mountain—I say who goes up it."

Meanwhile, Terry was totally focused on the hole they had dug.

"Look at this hole, Jamie. Isn't it great?" Terry asked. "We can make it deeper and deeper. Put a few boards on top and it can be an underground clubhouse, a hiding place, a trap for catching wild animals, or a place to hide treasures. Isn't it awesome?"

Jamie pointed to the mountain. "A mountain is better than a hole."

"Is not."

"Is so!"

"You can do more things with a hole," Terry said.

"No way!" said Jamie. "There are lots more things you can do on a mountain."

Terry climbed out of the hole and pulled Jamie's legs out from under him.

The two wrestled…hitting, pulling, and arguing all through it. Jamie managed to roll over and Terry tumbled into the hole, grabbing Jamie's shirt as he went. Jamie came tumbling after him. They landed side by side in the hole, covered with dirt.

The boys began to laugh. "Okay. The mountain and the hole are both fun," said Jamie.

And they went back to digging.

The Lesson

Many religious traditions profess the importance of "emptying." It is in letting go (emptying) that we make room for insight and awareness (fullness). Emptiness is a wondrous gift. The mountain can be a metaphor for rising above the commonplace and changing one's perspective. The fullness of a widening perspective is also a gift.

As parents we sometimes feel "emptied" by the constant giving. When you feel empty, take a moment to slow down and realize you are also being filled with a mountain of love!

Living the Lesson

Just for today, just for this moment, practice zazen. Just sit. Release all thoughts. Hear the sounds in your environment. Focus on the sound that is furthest away. Then switch your focus to the next sound. Then the one a bit closer.

Let the attention be on the sounds for a moment. Attend to each sound and then release that attention. Finally, focus on the sound of your breath. As you become immersed in the sounds of your breathing, all other sounds and focuses fade away. And then release all sounds. What is left is the emptiness. Nothing. No thing.

Expect nothing. Just be still in the emptiness. Make room for fullness.

Zen Magic: The Ordinary vs. Extraordinary

Eight-year-old Sally's eyes were focused on a spot of neon red in the field next to her house. She ran to see what it was. The Thing was round and when she picked it up it was soft to the touch. The Thing was speckled with tiny holes and had the bright red spot only on one side. She imagined it was a piece of a flying saucer or perhaps a magic machine. If she squeezed it she would become small or big. She closed her eyes and squeezed the Thing. In her mind, she was instantly transformed into a girl the size of a bug.

Just then her mother appeared over her. Sally was afraid she was too small for her mother to see. Maybe she would step on her and squash her. "Why are you holding onto that old rubber ball?" asked her Mom. "Please throw it in the garbage and go wash your hands."

The Lesson

What you see is what you get! Children know this lesson. Believing an old piece of rubber is a magic machine allows a child to explore creative thinking. Similarly, children respond to a parent's image of them. When we believe a child is "gifted" he will live up to that image. With inner eyes, the child senses the image in the mind of the adult. And, wanting to please, the child performs accordingly. This is the magic of life—the image held in the mind can become real. The ordinary can become extraordinary.

Every child lives in a world of the ordinary and extraordinary. Too many adults are stuck in the world of the ordinary. But, we all crave the extraordinary. By nurturing this paradox, parents can help increase a child's creativity and joy. What we attend to

57

will expand. What we ignore tends to fade into the background. Children can learn that the world has room for magic. It is best for us to remember it, too.

Living the Lesson

Look into a mirror with your child. Try to be poetic in your explanations of what you see. Look for a little magic. For example: "Your upper lip looks like the strong sail of a boat. Your eyes hold the fresh sparkle of dewdrops." After you have done this for each other, say the same things about yourself, "My upper lip looks like the strong sail of a boat..." (It's okay to laugh at your descriptions. My friend says my nose looks like a radish and my lips look like cracked mud!)

zen
discipline

Chapter 5

People who hate trouble generally get a good deal of it. —Harriet Beecher Stowe

Like the other sets of apparent opposites discussed in the previous chapter, authority and freedom are two parts of a whole. Authority and freedom must be balanced in childhood if children are to become self-assured adults who aren't imprisoned in their minds. To strike a balance, as parents we need to use our authority to set guidelines and steer the child to social responsibility, while also offering freedom to explore, create, and make choices.

A punitive authority figure will turn children into resentful conformists or mindless rebels, while a guiding authority can teach children their place in the world. Children then become responsible and contributing members of society.

Too much freedom is equally scary. Children who do not have the guidance of true authority figures are lost. They become prisoners of the mind, as they feel pulled by primitive impulses and sensations. Without guidance in how to tame those inner instincts and the roller coaster of emotions, they are at the mercy of whims. Is this true freedom? The real meaning of freedom is to find inner peace, despite outer circumstances.

The Buddha's gift to the world was to show us that life is suffering, and we are totally imprisoned by this suffering until we learn to tame the mind and its impulse to push us here and there, forever dissatisfied. To accomplish this kind of freedom children need discipline. In this book we define "authority" as a guiding force helping children find ways to control urges, impulses, and emotions. We look at "responsibility" as the gift children learn from appropriate discipline; it is "an ability to respond" without fears and anticipation.

Children must learn the following things from their parents:

- ✿ to act responsibly
- ✿ to work effectively
- ✿ to nurture and share with integrity
- ✿ to understand how to cope with change, loss, and fears
- ✿ to communicate effectively

These lessons are learned from the limits we set and the consequences we enforce in the moment when the child needs to hear them. It takes courage to speak the truth, especially in the presence of strangers who may witness our authority, and in the face of children who are feeling defiant and unhappy.

Consider how you determine the consequences for behavior that is inappropriate. Sometimes it is helpful to write down ideas as reminders and affirmations. Here are some examples:

* I will enforce appropriate consequences for inappropriate actions.
* I will be decisive and fair in my actions as my child's teacher.
* I will do my best to ensure that my child grows up to be responsible and well-mannered.
* I will correct myself as soon as possible when I do not act responsibly as my child's teacher and will right my mistake and commit to doing a better, more conscious job in the future.
* I will teach my child, through my actions, to understand that it is important to say, "I am sorry" and "I don't know."

Zen Butterflies

When I was eight, I discovered a great truth. On my way to school, I walked past the vacant lot where we played baseball after school. There, I saw millions of butterflies. Little flashing wings hovered like a great yellow blanket over the entire area.

I was in awe. Then, I heard the warning bell...five minutes to get to school or be tardy. It would mean having to stay after school in the principal's office if I didn't appear in my classroom in the next few minutes. I turned and started to run as fast as I could. After about a half block, I skidded to a stop.

To this day I remember the details of my thoughts at that moment. "What can they really do to me? Make me stay after school? Big deal. Watching the butterflies is much more important to me." And so, I returned to the butterfly

61

*world, captivated by their spring dance. About 15
minutes later, I walked quietly to school.
As I sat on the hard wooden bench outside the
principal's office that afternoon, I knew it had been
worth it. The field of fluttering yellow is forever
emblazoned on my mind. I had learned that I could do
what I thought best if I was willing to accept the
consequences.*

The Lesson

We must accept responsibility for our actions.

To this day I marvel that my eight-year-old mind figured out
such wisdom:

1. Don't miss the beauty of the moment.
2. If you're willing to accept the consequences of your actions,
you have nothing to fear.
3. "They" have no power that isn't given to them by you.

I'm proud of that little boy who figured out and then retained
such insights. This wisdom has guided me for many years and
has strengthened me to face some difficult choices.

This is a powerful lesson to teach children. Let's teach them to
accept the consequences for their actions. Spilled the milk?
Clean it up. Stole a friend's toy? Return it and buy an extra one
so there's double restitution. Want to watch the butterflies
instead of being on time? Stay after school. Accept it. You made
the trade off. All of life's choices have consequences.
Understanding this helps us determine our actions and
priorities.

Living the Lesson

This day, vow to begin teaching your children that all actions have consequences and, as long as they accept the consequences, they are free to take the action (obviously, dangerous actions are not acceptable). Mull this idea over in your mind. You'll begin to see that teaching responsibility by creating an awareness of consequences actually helps children develop the kind of discernment that will be of great value for the rest of their lives.

A Zen Look at Three Tries and Still No Success

"You look pretty today, Mom," said the young girl as she watched her mother tuck a new denim shirt into her pants. Mom looked up in surprise. Her child rarely gave compliments and she wasn't even trying to dress up. Then she remembered. "Thanks, dear. And the answer to the party question is still 'no.' There won't be enough supervision at Clara's house."

The daughter stormed out of the room. Then she came back to say, "You actually look like crap today. I lied."

The mom said, "Well, I'm sorry that's how you see it. I feel good and that's all that matters. And, no, you still can't go to the sleepover."

The daughter put on her best pout and hung her head and said, "You never let me do anything."

63

Her mother smiled and said, "Pouting won't work either, dear. I'm going next door to see the neighbor's new puppy. Would you like to join me?"

The girl did not answer and continued to pout until she heard the front door open and close. Then she ran to the door and shouted, "Hey! Wait for me."

The Lesson

This incident illustrates three "ploys" that children sometimes use to get what they want. First is the flattering approach. Next is the "make Mom feel bad" approach. Finally, comes the pouting, and the "you never let me do anything" guilt approach. The wonderful thing about this situation was that the mother did not get caught up in the child's drama. She remained calm and she stuck with her decision.

Some parents have shifted away from the "Parent-as-Authority" model in favor of the "Parent-as-Buddy" approach. However, when we try to treat our children as friends, we usually undermine our own authority and end up surrendering the most important parental responsibilities to teachers and others. Our children simply won't regard us as authority figures. When parents can be clear-headed about the job at hand and perform it—without expectations—then they can feel some sense of inner satisfaction.

The mother in the story saw the need to set a limit for her daughter. She believed a sleepover at Clara's house was a bad idea. And she faced her daughter's three tries to get past that limit. Had she felt unsure in her role, she might have given in. Children need to know the limits. And that can be pretty confusing in today's world in which so many politicians, movie stars, sports heroes, and next-door neighbors live as though there are no limits.

The daughter in this story learned that someone was looking out for her—a boundary was set. The world became safer and more manageable for her in that moment, although she didn't know it at the time.

As parents, we learn that the rewards of this job are mostly internal—not simply good feelings exchanged with a buddy. When we know we are being consistent and teaching strong values, when we are telling the truth and trying to be fair, then it doesn't matter if the outer rewards are there.

Living the Lesson

Begin by finding a quiet place to enter into the stillness. Sit with your back straight. Breathe deeply. Think only of breathing. Thoughts will come into your mind. Let them enter…let them leave. Don't grab hold of those stray thoughts. Watch your mind with interest, as if it were under a microscope. One thought swims in and wiggles its way out. Breathe and relax.

After you have spent some time focusing on breathing and releasing the mind chatter, see the word "Parent" in your mind. Focus on the letters, then on the sound of the word. Let the word fill you as if you were the word—as if you were the letters, the sound, the word, p-a-r-e-n-t. For this moment appreciate yourself in this role.

Now, let your mind be still again. Release expectations. Allow yourself to be still and learn to love the silence.

Zen Discipline

66 The Freedom of Zen

Maria had a "free day." She didn't have to go to school and her parents were both working.

"Mom, I'm 16. I can handle staying home alone for a few hours," Maria had insisted that morning.

Knowing her daughter as she did, Maria's mother agreed.

But by 11 a.m. all Maria had done was eat and watch television. Her hours of freedom were slipping away and she felt bored. Her friends were busy and she had nothing to do.

She wanted to enjoy her freedom. "Do something!" she told herself. So, she walked to the mall. She stopped at a fast-food restaurant to eat. Then she tried on clothes. She still felt bored.

Walking home, she saw a sprawling oak tree at the edge of the park. It seemed to be blocking her way for a reason. She hadn't climbed a tree in years and had an overwhelming desire to try to climb this one. She looked around furtively, not wanting anyone to see her do such a "childish" thing.

She climbed, pulling herself up higher and higher. It felt good. The tree was warm and oddly comforting. She found a spot where she could lean her back against the trunk and look down through the leaves into the park. A group of children and two women came loaded down with a picnic basket and balls. The children ran off and the two mothers sat down right below Maria. She could hear bits and pieces of their conversation. She closed her eyes and blocked out the world. Time disappeared. When she opened her eyes it was getting late.

That evening, Maria's mother asked what she had done with her day.

Maria said, "Mom, it was hard at first. I couldn't seem to find anything to do. Everything seemed pointless. But then I found out that I could just sit and be quiet. And that was great. Isn't that strange?"

Maria's mom just smiled.

The Lesson

Like Maria, we tend to fill our lives with distractions. But what are we distracting ourselves from? What are we trying not to see? The mind prison wants us to fill up with things and worries and plans. It keeps us craving newness. That way, we avoid the place in the mind that is most scary. It is the emptiness that we avoid.

Yet, it is in the emptiness that we find the opportunity to be filled up by something other than distracting cravings. True satisfaction is really what we are looking for when we talk about wanting freedom. And this deep satisfaction comes from facing the emptiness and slowly letting ourselves release into the Oneness. In the emptiness, where the cravings of the worldly self do not exist, we find that we are full.

Satisfaction and true freedom come only when we quiet the mind. Maria found out she could be free in the quiet she created. She was able to do this because she had developed an

67

inner discipline and inner authority. That guidance kept her from trying destructive distractions. That guidance urged her to trust herself when she saw the tree. In that moment, Maria found a balance of freedom and authority.

Living the Lesson

Try the following craft exercise. You will need:

- ✿ a box with a lid
- ✿ magazines
- ✿ old jewelry
- ✿ glue
- ✿ markers
- ✿ paint
- ✿ a mirror to fit inside the box

Begin by pasting on the outside of the box all of the things you distract yourself with, including food, money, clothing, work, and other material things that occupy your mind. Then along the inside of the box write, "God is where? God is here. Answers are here." Paste the mirror on the bottom of the box.

Outside there is busyness. Inside there is emptiness. Where do we find the freedom we seek? Inside.

Face yourself.

work is zen

Chapter 6

The reward of a thing well done is to have done it.

—Emerson's Essays,
New England Reformers

Work is love made visible.

—Kahil Gibran, *The Prophet*

When children are taught to appreciate the value of applying themselves to achieve "a thing well done," they grow to become adults who know how to find meaning and satisfaction in work. They will find their lives are less filled with suffering when they are occupied in life-sustaining efforts.

Work exists, in its essence, as a way to gather food and provide shelter. Zen masters believe all people should participate in some way towards producing these things. It is a necessity, a basic reality. Life is not sustained without work. And to allow someone else to sustain your life because of laziness is not Zen.

Work can and should be self-gratifying rather than done grudgingly in order to earn the money for some future fulfillment.

70   Psychologists talk about the importance of being able to "delay gratification" because in many aspects of life, we must wait in order to reach a goal or feel a reward. But, in fact, what we really need to learn as adults, and find ways to teach our children, is that we can feel gratitude for each moment. Often we don't have control over what is contained in the moments of our lives. But we can control how we react to these moments. We have total control over our attitude and through our attitude, we have some limited control over the things we draw into our lives. We have control over our ability to "find gratification." That is the Zen of psychology—find gratification in everything. It need not be delayed!

Zen Desserts

Brigit wanted to help with supper. At age four, her idea of "helping" was usually pouring water into bowls, grabbing anything else she could get her hands on, and then stirring to see how much could be splashed onto the counter and floor! But I appreciated her enthusiasm and didn't want to squelch her interest in helping out.

I told Brigit, "When I was a girl, my job at suppertime was fixing desserts. My mom said, 'If you want desserts every night, you can make them. I don't have time.' And, because she was raising six children, I knew that was true. So I became 'the dessert girl.' I learned to be very clever at making something from nothing because my father never bought things you could use to make desserts when he went for the groceries."

I suggested to Brigit that she could become a "dessert girl." I got out three frozen piecrusts. One was to hold our dinner—a quiche—I was in charge of that one. The other two were for her to use in her very first dessert experiment. I set out sugar, cinnamon, nutmeg, butter, chocolate chips, and peanut butter and she dreamed up her own concoctions.

She dictated her recipe to me. "In one crust you put sugar on the bottom—just sprinkles, 'cause too much will rot your teeth. Then put spice and butter. Mix them up. But be careful. Don't get spice in the butter jar or your sandwich will be yucky tomorrow! Then add peanut butter. Smoosh it all around the bottom. This is hard, Mom, because it keeps scrunching onto the sides. The other one gets sugar on the bottom and chocolate chips. You can only have small pieces because it's very sweet so it'll also rot your teeth. Some butter is good too, just because it's yummy. Put it in the oven and you're done!!"

We cooked her creations alongside the quiche—they browned into perfectly interesting tarts in a short time. After our supper, we enjoyed Brigit's original desserts with ice cream.

The Lesson

Children who are allowed to enjoy working will grow up to know that all work can be a source of pleasure and fulfillment. "Work" is defined here as "concentrated effort for a specific purpose." Brigit concentrated on making a dessert that everyone would enjoy and that would nourish us. She succeeded in contributing in a meaningful way to the family dinner.

72 To concentrate, whether it is in making a family meal or while using a hammer and nails, is a Zen process. In concentrating your whole being on the activity at hand, you stop the worrying, judging, fantasizing, or any of the other distractions that create suffering. Thus, work can be a sacred activity. Work allows us to release the past, the future, our judgments, and our fears by putting us squarely within the present moment. We become united with the effort and the things we are creating. In such activities we contribute to our own well-being and to the well-being of others.

Children have a natural ability to merge with what they are doing and be fully present in the moment. If children are given real-life projects to focus on, they will fully embrace the chance to contribute to the world. And when parents nurture these work efforts, our children may very well retain, for life, the ability to find deep satisfaction in putting forth effort for the betterment of home and world. And that's important since work is the "dessert" and substance of life.

It is best to learn the value of focusing one's efforts on the things at hand during the years of childhood.

Living the Lesson

Children should have "chores" to do on a regular basis. Plan a list of regular chores for every member of the family. Below are some "work" activities that even young children can do and feel they are helping the family. If work is defined as "a physical contribution to the well-being of all," then it becomes very satisfying.

- ✿ Water the plants.
- ✿ Scrub the sink.
- ✿ Feed the pets.

- ❧ Make the sandwiches.
- ❧ Set the table.
- ❧ Wash the dishes.
- ❧ Put laundry in the laundry room.
- ❧ Sweep the floor.
- ❧ Vacuum.
- ❧ Create a "Zen dessert."

Zen Jobs

Once, a woman had a job she loved. She looked forward to going to work. She answered phones and waited on customers. She was known as the "problem solver." The other employees looked up to her. When she went home after work, she still had energy to enjoy her children and fulfill her role as a mother. In the evenings, she read to her children and helped them with homework.

Then, the management changed. New employees were hired. At lunchtime, some employees brought in a TV and watched soap operas. She felt the disdainful looks from the others when she did not join in on the new routine. She felt the hostility from others as they worked as little as possible and wanted her to slow down. Work became painful. She no longer had answers to problems. She no longer went home with energy. She had no patience with her children. The joy had gone out of life.

One rainy day on the way to work, her car skidded off the road. She wasn't hurt but she was scared, and she had an "a-ha" epiphany. She realized her life was miserable and she understood that she had become a negative force in the lives of her children. The next day, she decided it was time to find new work that she could enjoy and that's exactly what she did. She hadn't studied Zen but she knew, instinctively, that work is to be a blessing to yourself and others. She decided it was time to make a change and regain the joy of living.

The Lesson

Work should be a positive flow of energy. When parents honor their own call to "change the things that can be changed," children learn the lesson of the Serenity Prayer:
God grant me the Serenity to accept the things I cannot change, the Courage to change the things I can, and the Wisdom to know the difference.

Living the Lesson

Working with art materials is, for many, an act of courage. This is especially true for those who believe they have no talent. When you reach out with courage and make an effort to create something on paper you have "changed the thing (paper) that can be changed." After you find the courage to act, you need to find the serenity to accept what you have created (the art) and that is the beginning of wisdom.

For today, try this experiment:

Using water-based markers, draw a picture of a face—it is the face of courage. Then, using a brush and a little bit of water, lightly stroke the face on the page. The edges will bleed. The picture is transformed. Such is life. We do what we can. But, then, *life* takes over.

Do this with your children and talk about the lessons of the Serenity Prayer. After the pictures are dry, remember that you can still use black to add details that may have become blurred. Thus, if you are troubled by what is before you, you can take action to change it.

Life Is Work—Hooray!!

Right after Mary got home from school with her children she said, "It's time to take care of the animals, and I need some help pulling weeds in the garden."

Karen, the oldest, went outside immediately to bring hay to the horse and then to clean his stall. But her sister Elizabeth said, "Why do I have to do all the work?"

Mary answered with a glint of mischief in her eye. "You want to do all the work? That would be really great! Thanks for offering. Here are a few things to start with: the dishes are waiting, the laundry needs to be done, and don't forget to scrub the kitchen floor and run to the store to get groceries for supper. Oh, yes, your sister goes to dance class at six. And, please look for a good job soon, the bills are piling up."

75

Elizabeth ran out to the garden, laughing, "Okay, okay! I get it, Mom. Are you coming too?"

"Sure am," she said, smiling.

The Lesson

In today's world, "work" has become a negative word. A noble word and concept masks an underlying problem. Our youth are not coached enough by parents, teachers, and others to view work as a means to self-fulfillment as opposed to a means to an end.

It is focused work and an attitude of appreciation for the moment that create a full life. There's the old story of the gardener who had produced a lush and prolific garden. A friend stopped by and said, "God has certainly blessed you with a bountiful harvest." The gardener said, "Yes, he has. But you should have seen it when God had it by Himself." There's a clear message here: The garden was flourishing because of the sweat on the man's brow. Work, struggle, and discipline are absolutely necessary to bring about good results.

The purpose of visualization and meditation is not to imagine things appearing from out of the blue. Visualization—in a Zen context—is to see the reality around you as beautiful and useful despite outward appearances. Meditation means to still the mind and focus only on the breath (or the candle, or the moment). Both visualization and meditation are disciplines, requiring concerted, daily effort. And over time, both will bring great clarity to life.

Meditation is not an excuse to drop out of the world or to stop working. The Buddha meditated for many years. It was his "work" and it took great focus and effort. From his meditations the Buddha came to see that what causes suffering are our interpretations, anticipations, expectations, and an unwillingness to embrace change. When we can release these things and go with the flow of life, then, and only then, will suffering end.

Focused work, which is a discipline, can help free the mind from suffering.

Living the Lesson

Wash the dishes in the sink tonight even if you have a dishwasher. Do it as a meditation. Feel the water on your hands. Feel the warmth. Feel the soap. Feel the slipperiness of the washcloth on the plate. See the plate sparkle. Hear the water as you add it to the rinse tub. Feel the water rinsing away the final particles of soap. With each plate feel, see, hear, and be.

It is a discipline to concentrate on the work at hand. And, concentrating on the moment, with its sensory input, is a spiritual act. To be one with the water and the plates and the soap—without separation—allows a feeling of *transcendence*. We become one with the One.

Children learn more from your example than your words. Don't grouse about what needs to be done. Do it wholeheartedly and with joy.

zen during divorce

Some people enjoy being negative. They enjoy criticizing, blaming and attacking...(But) being negative is not heroic or intelligent.
—Edward DeBono,
Handbook for the Positive Revolution

When we face the emptiness that comes along with big life changes, such as divorce, we have a great opportunity because it is exactly in these empty moments that insights and growth occur. When we can accept this time of endings and new beginnings, we open the door for true enlightenment.

For Siddhartha (who was to become the Buddha) there were long periods of total emptying as he sat under the Bodhi tree. During his years of meditation, he was tormented by dark temptations. He struggled with his wandering mind. Then he let go. He embraced emptiness. And in those times of releasing and facing the darkness with courage, he became the Awakened One—the Buddha.

80 Now, let's take a look at how times of struggle—such as a divorce—can become an opportunity for great insight. When parents go through this crisis, the children may also feel they are being submerged in darkness and chaos. The best way to help them is to model how to walk out of darkness into the light.

Even if you are not faced with divorce, use this chapter to consider what it means for you and for your children to deal with big changes. These might include moving to a new town, changing schools, a serious illness in the family, dealing with/understanding violence in the community and the world, or dealing with a new job or a loss of income.

The Troubled Times

She was divorced 20 years ago and felt grateful for the years of tension and litigation, which strengthened her. She used the difficult years in a very Zen way; she didn't hide from them, she experienced them. And, because she did, they prepared her for work as a counselor. In earlier years, she never knew she would be able to counsel and guide others, helping people use their spiritual resources to deal with their troubles. In addition, her children had grown into smart and strong women. But she remembers the years of chaos.

She said, "Every day my ex affected my life, bringing fear and concerned anticipation about what he'd do next. We were divorced; I had sole custody. But still he made hate-filled phone calls. He took the children and didn't bring them back on time. He threatened not to bring them back at all."

"We were in court over and over about child support issues and visitation. Things didn't change for 10 years and during that time I often found myself hoping that he would move far away, or even die. And then I felt guilty for even thinking such things. A judge forced him to pay back the child support he owed. He was on his way out of town when he dropped off the check to me. When my lawyer and I arrived at the bank we found out he had written the full amount he owed in the numerical part, but in the written part of the check the amount was in tens, instead of thousands. It was his final 'gotcha.'"

Because she went through those years of turmoil, she learned to speak her mind, stick up for herself, trust in God, and recognize her strengths. Her daughters grew up, married, and had children of their own.

The Lesson

Some people do not know how to let go and some don't want to. In divorce situations, this is especially hurtful, but also very common. It is a sign of maturity to know when to release the past and the people in it. It is the sign of true adulthood to be able to step into the void and create something new.

This story shows what happens in situations in which one parent initiates a change (divorce), but then can't accept it. This father could neither find a graceful new way to coexist nor could he move on with his life while maintaining some dignity.

Yet, the mother found great strength and courage despite the years of pain and insecurity. She was able to move from the past to the present. The lesson is that we can endure—when that is the only option. And we can persevere with courage and grace. And as always, we must simply accept what is.

81

82   Living the Lesson

When life is most chaotic it is helpful to find ways to control the wandering mind. Try these things to keep your mind focused on the present rather than being invaded by the past or future:

- ✿ listen to music
- ✿ sing songs
- ✿ journal—write down observations of the immediate moment

Learn to pay attention to the thoughts in your mind. When negative self-talk arises, do not reach out and grab hold; let it pass into and out of your mind. This takes practice!

Children of Divorce

Jessica and Laura had been friends since preschool. They had walked to school every day for five years. Now, in fourth grade, their friendship, and Jessica's life, seemed to be falling apart. Jessica's mom tried to tell her everything would be all right.

"Mom, you don't understand," Jessica said. "She doesn't want to be my friend anymore."

The nine-year-old rushed into the bathroom and closed the door. A few minutes later when Jessica's mom went to check on her, she opened the door just in time to see Jessica swallowing a pill. It was Tylenol. Her daughter said, "It helps me calm down."

"Jessica," her mom said. "I don't ever want you to take medicine without my permission. That is meant for physical pain. It's not the answer to your problems."

"I knew you wouldn't understand. It's all your fault anyway," her daughter screamed and then burst into tears as she ran out of the house. Jessica's mom ran after her, caught her, and held on. She held on tight because now her own hot tears were welling up. How had she missed her daughter's turmoil?

She knew things had been hard for Jessica since the divorce but she'd been so busy trying to keep herself together that she had believed her daughter was coping pretty well. They had to move and no longer lived next door to Laura. And the apartment they were in was small and didn't allow pets so they had given their cat to Laura. And every other weekend her daughter was at her dad's house, although she complained that she didn't want to go. But overall, Jessica had seemed okay.

"Tell me how you feel, Jessica. Please tell me," her mother said through her tears.

As they walked home holding on to each other, Jessica told of her experience. She explained how Laura had become more distant because Jessica didn't have as much time to spend with her. She told how Laura and several other girls were on a baseball team that Jessica couldn't join because she spent half the summer at her

83

*father's house on the other side of town. She told her
mom about the time her Dad walked her into school
and the other girls laughed at her as though she were in
kindergarten. She explained how painful it was when
Laura and her new friends gossiped about Jessica. She
let her mom know she was missing birthday parties
because she spent weekends away. And, finally, she
said her step-mom criticized almost everything she did
or said.*

*Her mother was overwhelmed. She had no idea. She
apologized to Jessica for not being in touch with what
was going on in her life.*

The Lesson

All parents make mistakes. What can we do to rectify these
mistakes? Keep coming back to the moment. Return our
attention to the here-and-now. Surrender our problems and
tension. Remember the children. You can see from this story
that the mother knew what to do once she entered the
moment. She hugged her daughter. She talked with her about
her problems. She asked for forgiveness.

Living the Lesson

From a Zen perspective, there are several ways to help children
of divorce:

❀ Pay attention. Be available. Notice in what ways the
changes have had an impact on friendships, school
performance, and frustration levels.

❀ Model forgiveness and gentleness and these qualities
will be passed on to the child. Sometimes it means

using the words "Let go," or "Time to move on" as a continual and subliminal mantra to be said over and over when you feel angry at an ex-spouse. For the sake of the children, there must be forgiveness.

❁ Teach the children a four-step process for solving problems: First, express the feelings without acting on them, by journaling, talking, and so on. Second, release the feelings—by breathing into them and saying, "Let go." Third, brainstorm (and write down) all possible answers to the problem including those that seem silly or unrealistic. Fourth, release the problem. Surrender it into the Great Emptiness. Guidance will come in time. Ideas will appear. Your child will know what to do.

❁ Share daily magical moments by taking nature walks with your child. The earth is a great healer. Notice rocks, trees, birds, and sky. This world is here beneath us and in front of us—ready to lift away tension. The birds call out, "Life is not awful. It is awe-filled." Teach your child how to have an "awe-filled" day.

The Zen of Divorce—Endings and Beginnings

I was in the throes of divorce while trying to cope with the meaning of being a single mom. I didn't want to let my young children know how scared and sad I felt. So I asked my four-year-old son to take a walk with me. We put the baby in the backpack and headed out into the sagebrush.

In front of our house there was a long, never-ending field of coarse scrub. It seemed a lonely, desolate place on that day. But on other days it seemed freeing and expansive.

As we walked, I let my son do the talking. He said, "You have a sore throat, mommy." I was surprised. I didn't feel sick—but emotionally I knew the words I needed to say were stuck in my throat. I said, "Thank you for saying that. You're right."

Just as we began heading home, he said, "You need this piece of wood." He picked it up and gave it to me. It was a twisted knothole piece from a cedar tree that hadn't survived on this harsh open mesa. I told him it looked rotten.

"You can carve it, Mommy," he said.

"But it's too heavy to carry all the way home," I lied as I tossed it on the ground. In fact, it wasn't heavy at all. Bugs had eaten out the center.

Quietly, he picked it up and carried it home for me. That night, as my children slept, I cried over that piece of wood. It certainly didn't look like it should be anything but firewood, but I felt like chopping at something.

I took a butter knife and started to pound it into the wood. I chopped and cried, I dug into the rottenness. By morning I had scraped away all of the old wood. What remained was a beautiful shell. The outer lines swirled in cosmic directions. It was becoming a work of art.

That afternoon I felt an urge to paint the hollow part within. I mixed a dark gray color and began pouring it into the crevices. I still felt as if I was playing at destruction rather than creation. At any moment I was sure I would throw this wooden piece into the fireplace.

But when the wood had dried, I saw that this hollowed piece was becoming an accurate reflection of my current state. With the paint, it looked as if this hollow vessel had survived a fire. What remained was still beautiful and strong. I created a small icon-like figure to hang on the inside. She is black with a full moon belly. Barely visible against the dark grays of the inside, she is my reminder that there is redemption—there is fullness even in the emptiness.

My son was the one who called me into this awareness. He was, and often is, the voice of Spirit. I reminded myself to never lie to him again—the piece of wood wasn't too heavy as I told him—it was my heart that was too heavy and his persistence helped lighten it.

88 The Lesson

In much of life, the same sequence unfolds: First, there is destruction, an ending, a death of some sort. Then comes the light, with all its insights and growth.

Is it necessary that endings come before beginnings? It seems to be the human predicament. We learn through making mistakes, and true growth and strength come after we have suffered. The lessons of the wood sculpture are two-fold.

First, we are stronger than we think. Reaching that place of emptiness is very powerful. It is during those times when our ego is devastated and our old self-definitions are no longer meaningful that we are able to go to a higher level and find new freedom. Most religions say that God comes in to fill the empty places. It is only when we are empty of Ego-answers that the Spirit-answers are able to come to us.

Second, our children are often the ones who guide us to the next level of awareness. When I was dealing with divorce, I couldn't hear my inner voice because I was too caught up in my "situation," but my son could hear. How did he do that? How did he know I was making my throat sore or that I needed to work with this special piece of wood? He knew because pure love transcends age, ego, and self-limitations.

What does this mean from a Zen perspective? Zen teaches us "not to fight the river." When we go with the flow and release ourselves to the "what is" of life, we can see the fullness that is there even in the emptiness. The fullness of life is the beauty, the abundance, the love, the opportunity, the grace that is always there. We are never far from wisdom. It is buried within. And when we empty ourselves of the clutter, that wisdom can reveal itself.

Living the Lesson

Try this meditation: Find a clear glass cup and set it in front of you. Allow yourself to look carefully at this empty container. Then imagine all of the things with which it could be filled. Picture each of the following items (or imagine your own list):

- ❀ See the glass filled with milk, then with water, then with grape juice.
- ❀ See the glass filled with flowers, with marbles, with some love letters, with torn pictures.
- ❀ See the glass filled with straws, with scissors, with pencils and markers.
- ❀ See the glass filled again with flowers.

Now look again at the empty container. See the glass as it sparkles in the light. See the rim as it defines the edges. Appreciate the crisp emptiness. It is this very essence that allows for infinite possibilities. Close your eyes and release all images. Release everything. Become empty. Trust the emptiness. There is healing there. Nothing needs to happen. All is perfect in the moment.

The Ex-Spouse

She had been divorced for five years but he still wanted to control her life. At the time of the divorce, she had no idea that this might go on and on. Although the marriage had ended because of their poor communication, it became even worse after the divorce.

He refused to talk to her directly, but he pumped the children for information and then sent threatening notes insisting on changes.

At one point, she sent him a note offering her observations about the children's health. She received a message from him, stating that he planned to file an order with the court regarding the health issues. He offered no explanation.

She fumed over the note, feeling righteous indignation. Then she sat down to meditate and let it go. As she tried to see the exasperation disappearing, a light began to dawn. She realized that she could strip away the threats and the bullying and go to the small kernel of concern. Obviously, the note meant he was worried even if he couldn't say it.

When she got to this point, she laughed. He seemed like a small child throwing a tantrum, and she had spent the last two days behaving in a similar fashion. Because of her new clarity, she was able to approach the situation with maturity and without bitterness and rage.

The Lesson

Divorce requires a lot of letting go and readjusting. Many times, we think that the problems of a marriage will go away once the divorce is final. But, if there are children involved, many couples learn that the problems have actually multiplied! Troubles in communication and joint decision-making don't usually go away. An important lesson in this process is to continually release bad feelings about the ex-spouse and focus on the children. Another lesson is to let go of the feeling, "I shouldn't have to deal with these kind of situations anymore."

Life is what it is. Wishing it were different or being indignant doesn't change anything. What we can do is use a few effective tools to help navigate these turbulent waters.

Tool 1: Let go of expectations and unfulfilled dreams. The past is gone. Try to keep it out of the present.

Tool 2: Stay focused on what is possible to accomplish right now. Try to communicate without emotion as if you were talking politely to a stranger. Keep the conversation on specifics regarding the children. Don't make small issues into battles.

Tool 3: Give up the drama. Stories about an ex-spouse make for colorful conversation with family and friends. It incites their anger and inspires them to share their stories. However, this replaying of injustices helps keep them alive. The memory of wrongdoing can be felt over and over. Try to minimize the storytelling to include only those times when you need input on what to do next. Try releasing pent-up feelings by journaling, walking, and creating artwork.

Living the Lesson

Positive self-talk is helpful when we are dealing with big life changes and ongoing problems. To re-program yourself to avoid becoming caught up in the drama of life, and to respond with full attention to the children, try the following tool. Create an audiotape for yourself. On the tape play some soothing background music as you repeat the following phrases to use:

❀ I am focusing on the moment. I am in the moment. I am seeing all that is here now. I am smelling, tasting, touching, feeling, hearing…I am in my body and my body is sitting here—now.

❀ I release all that is other than the now. I release the drama. I am letting go. As I breathe in I take in the healing breath of life. As I breathe out I release the dark clouds of pain.

❀ I am able to respond to each day as it unfolds. I will do what needs to be done right now without indecision or fear. I am response-able. I am responding to life right here, right now. And that is all I need to do for the moment.

❀ Challenge your child to a race. Feel the wind in your hair. Feel your muscles expanding. Allow emotions to drain away and enjoy laughing about winning or losing.

hellos
and
goodbyes

Chapter 8

My religion is to live—and die—without regret.
—Milarepa
from *The Tibetan Book of Living and Dying*

Death is inevitable yet it is one of the most
feared and fiercely avoided realities any of us
will have to face. In the west we say we will
"rage, rage against the dying of the light." We
struggle to thwart death. How is it possible to
accept the loss of relatives, family members,
friends, or even pets and jobs? How do we help
children deal with the difficult issues of grief
and loss?

In Buddhism, it is recognized that making peace
with death is necessary before we are truly free
to live without fear and thus, to end suffering.
(See *The Tibetan Book of Living and Dying* by
Sogyal Rinpoche.) Buddhism recognizes that
death is inevitable and as such, it is a "what is" of
life. We need to accept that it will come. Denial
creates a barrier to living in the moment. How
can you appreciate the preciousness of today if

you believe there will be endless tomorrows in which to pay better attention?

Ancient masters teach that beginnings and endings are inexplicably intertwined. When a baby is born, that infant experiences an end to its life in the womb. Then comes the beginning of a life that is separate from the mother. As the child grows he will experience many endings—for example, the end of one school year, the end of a relationship with that teacher. These endings will give way to a new year and a new teacher. Throughout life the child will face the loss of family members, friends, pets, and other endings, as well as major life changes. To help alleviate the tragic feelings associated with these events, learn to observe the natural world.

The ocean waves wash up with fullness and recede into emptiness. The seasons go from the freezing, deathlike qualities of winter into the blossoming newness of spring. In watching these things we can learn to welcome the new day each morning and say good-bye to it at night. We need to teach our children to observe and find appreciation for the daily comings and goings of life. The grand pattern of hellos and good-byes is repeated over and over in all of life.

This awareness doesn't take away the pain that comes with loss. But it does make it more understandable and easier to bear over time. In this chapter we share stories about several children who have died. This is the ultimate tragedy for a parent—to outlive a child. And yet, all of these children coped with impending death in heroic ways and saw themselves as teachers. Their stories are shared here to help shed light on the gift we call "life." It is exactly because life ends that it is precious. The presence of death reminds us to celebrate what we have right here, right now.

The Zen of Death

*Tasha was a sweet, loveable dog. When Peter was just
over one day old, I laid him in Tasha's comforting "lap."
Baby against dog belly; her dog face circled protectively
closer to his. That is what I remember. As Peter grew, he
would pull her tail and chase her, and she tolerated it all,
always graciously watching over the growing humans.
She was special because she was always there for us.*

*Six years later, Tasha's legs weren't working. She could no
longer stand up. The vet said her brain wasn't
communicating to her legs. How could this be? I carried
her outside two times a night to do her biological
business. During the day, I carried her outside so she
could rest under her favorite tree. Meanwhile, my young
daughter was still waking up at night, demanding
another kind of attention. My days were full, caring for
children and visiting the sick dog outside. Tasha's special
needs had to be squeezed in between other needs.*

*The vet said there was no cure for her condition. Maybe
she would get better. Maybe not. After taking her for that
visit she laid again under the tree. I watched her. She
looked around wildly. She wanted to get water and
couldn't. She wanted to nibble at her bowl but couldn't
get there. She wanted to go and cuddle with my daughter
who was toddling out to see her. But she couldn't move
anything but her head.*

*It was torture to decide what should happen next. I
didn't want to decide. She had been my ever-present
companion for years. But I had children to attend to. The
nighttime outings were exhausting. I dreamed I could do*

95

it all. To be with her and let the children see her die whenever that time was meant to be. But this was a time calling for a decision. No right or wrong, just clarity.

One morning I woke up feeling clear. Tasha needed relief from this life. It was time for an end to her suffering. I told the children she was dying and it was time to say goodbye. We did a ritual—singing for her and praying that we were doing the right thing. My son knew the right song to sing, "Sing your way home at the end of the day; Sing your way home, chase the shadows away..." We gave her a special drink and burned incense to ease her pain. Then we took her to the vet. He gave her a shot. Her head, which she always held high, drooped. She was gone.

After several weeks of her illness, death came too fast. It seemed incomprehensible. We cried. We buried her toys and treats in the back yard. We sang for her. Tasha was gone.

The Lesson

Death teaches many lessons. It is natural, despite our culture's attempts to defy it. Death comes to every creature. We have tried too hard to pretend it doesn't have to be. Death is a "what is." It happens, despite all resistance.

Children who see pets die, or who go to the funeral of a grandparent, or who visit the sick—these children learn about the cycle of life. We are born, we live, we struggle, we strive, we accept, and we die. Such is the essence of existence. When we accept this as reality we can more fully live in the moment. Life is rich and precious precisely because it has a beginning and an end.

Tasha was a dog that lived fully. Only one week before her illness began we went on a long walk. She didn't need a leash. She hopped agilely over creek beds. She chased rabbits but returned immediately when called. She pranced on the road. She was a happy, beautiful dog. In death, she was equally dignified.

Experiencing these times to the fullest is, perhaps, what is most crucial. Children need to know that death happens. It is a time to express a sadness and a heart-filled goodbye, which includes appreciating all that has been.

Living the Lesson

Practice saying goodbye to the day. Each night acknowledge that a day has ended. Be grateful for the opportunity of one day. Ask your child the following questions:

- ✿ What are you grateful for in this day?
- ✿ What did you do today that made the world a better place (how did you help someone else)?
- ✿ What do you appreciate about your life? (your family members, your school work, your animals, your house—pick one and consider specifics about each.)

These questions help us all focus on life as a gift and a responsibility. It is our sacred task to make the world a better place by our presence. Children love to make this questioning period a nightly ritual.

98 Zen Death Mask

Jake was in a drug treatment center. He had spent 10 of his 20 years intoxicated or high. He liked to be "happy," he said. I asked him to make a mask and showed him how to create a face. He played with the clay foundation. All of a sudden something seemed to capture his interest. He focused on his project. He was the first to finish a mask. It was the face of an old man.

"Who is he?" I asked. Jake did not want to say. I put the mask on and said, "Come on, Jake. Talk to me."

Jake told me that his grandfather, portrayed in the mask, had been his best friend as a young child. His grandfather had lived in the house across the street. Every morning Jake had eaten breakfast at home and then breakfast at Grandpa's. One day Jake headed out the door to go see his grandfather, but his mother stopped him.

"Grandpa's gone," she said. She was upset but didn't say anything else. After about a week of not seeing Grandpa, people came and began taking things out of Grandpa's house. The little boy asked again, "Where is Grandpa?"

Now his mom seemed angry. She said only, "He's gone and we aren't going to talk about him anymore."

For years the boy wondered if his grandfather hated him and had moved away. It wasn't until he was in school and heard others talking about people dying that Jake knew his grandfather had died. He had never been given the chance to say goodbye.

Jake used the mask as a way to say goodbye to his grandfather.

The Lesson

We think we should protect children from the reality of death. It seems scary and beyond comprehension. But the reality of an old person dying or a pet dying is simply a part of life that we must learn.

Living the Lesson

Let your children know that death happens. Give them opportunities to mourn and to say goodbye. Remember those who have died. Do rituals to mourn the loss of a pet. Sing songs. These things put death in perspective and help to move past sadness.

Offering service to people who are closer to death can help us find greater acceptance. And it is also true that "in giving we receive." So, take your children to visit a nursing home.

Children who are eight years old or older will benefit a great deal from talking to older people. Offer to be a volunteer, and visit those who are lonely. Offer to write down their stories. The older ones have a wealth of wisdom. When you do this, you open the door to a flood of loving kindness that flows out and returns.

Anna's Zen Story

Anna was diagnosed with an inoperable cancerous tumor on her brain stem when she was 10 years old. The doctors experimented with radiation treatments and steroids in a desperate attempt to save the little girl's life. But the medicines did little more than make Anna's deteriorating body bloat up like a whale. Her parents tried to prepare themselves—Anna didn't have long to live.

Despite the gloomy prognosis Anna wanted to go to school. She entered the sixth grade with a body her friends didn't recognize. She couldn't walk; she had trouble talking. But she laughed! Every moment with her friends was filled with the humor that transcends tragedy.

During that first week of school, her English teacher asked the students to write on the often-dreaded topic: What did you do on your summer vacation? Anna wrote this story; "I was fishing with my dad when I got dizzy. I had a headache, too. So, my parents took me to the doctor. He said I have a tumor on my brain. He gave me medicines that make me sick and made me get fat. The bad news is the doctor says I am going to die; but the good news is he says I don't have to go to gym class anymore!"

When I met Anna she was a silly 10-year-old girl flirting with an 11-year-old boy. But she was also a girl confined to a wheelchair who was attending my art therapy group on "Attitudinal Healing." She and her parents were looking for help and support to deal with the inevitable.

*In fact, it was her parents who were looking for help;
Anna came along for the ride! Somehow, she stayed
above it all. She especially liked the 11-year-old boy in the
group whose life expectancy wasn't much longer than
hers.*

*Anna drew rainbows and butterflies. She used a fluid
marker clutched between her chubby fingers. Despite her
choking voice box, she told jokes. I soon realized she and
the other children in the group didn't need any attitude
changes, but the parents did. Anna's parents, as any
parent can imagine, were angry; they wanted the cancer
to stop; they wanted to know "why?" They wanted more
time. The whole experience was unacceptable. Impossible.
Unforgivable.*

*As time progressed, their daughter taught them what
they needed to know…to live with gusto. In every
moment Anna lived, she was intense. She screamed when
she needed to and laughed hysterically as often as she
could. She had a clear sense of priorities.*

The Lesson

To deny death, as we so often do in this culture, means we
postpone life. We live as if we have endless time. "I will tell my
husband I love him tomorrow; and on Friday I'll spend some
quality time with Johnny." Tomorrow does not yet exist and
may choose not to appear.

Anna and her friends teach us to embrace today even when
the challenges seem overwhelming. There is a message, a lesson
to remember in every difficulty.

101

102 In an old Zen story, a great master dies and his student is asked, "What was the high point of your master's life?" The student replies, "Each moment he lived was the highest and best moment of his life."

So, when this particular hour of life seems difficult, remember, this hour is passing. Who knows what comes next? It is the law of impermanence. And in that void of not-knowing, in the great empty places of life, there is always a light.

Anna saw a benefit: "No more gym class!" What a gift to focus on the good news amidst the bad.

Living the Lesson

Buy a piece of modeling clay (or borrow it from your child). Make sure it is an oil-based clay that becomes more malleable as it is warmed in the hands. Close your eyes and hold the clay. Clear your mind. Release all thoughts, all anxieties into the clay. The clay will accept the messages of your fingers. See your tensions flowing down your arms, into your fingers, and then into the clay. Relax and release. Spend 10 minutes doing this clay meditation.

Now, open your eyes and look at the clay. It may demand to be created into a shape or it may already have a message to share. Allow yourself to see the feelings released into the clay.

Be present to all your emotions today. Acknowledge them and notice when they are present. And remember that everything passes. Nothing is permanent. That is a law of the universe.

Corey's Zen

*Corey's cancer was called a Wilm's Tumor. He had more
than 20 major surgeries in his 14 years of life. The scars
on his belly looked like a detailed map of back roads. His
teeth were rotting and his hearing was going. Yet, Corey
also insisted on going to school. He told other students,
"Don't laugh at me because I'm bald and talk funny. I'm
here, ain't I?"*

*When Corey was eight, he started to draw a series of
teddy bears. The drawings were a comfort to him.
Eventually, he drew them to comfort others. He drew his
friends and family as teddy bear characters. He entered
his drawings of "Invisible Bear" and "Blown-Apart Bear"
and "Lightning Bear" in art shows.*

*One day, I shared with him the story of President
Theodore Roosevelt's bear hunt:*

*"In 1902, Theodore (Teddy) Roosevelt wanted to go out
to the wild west and shoot a bear. So, his aides went to
the wooded mountains first and caught a wounded bear.
They tied it up and led the president to the spot where he
could shoot it and not be hurt in the process.*

*Theodore Roosevelt refused to shoot a wounded bear
already in captivity. The next morning the papers carried
cartoons about the failed bear hunt. They portrayed a
cute bear they called, "Teddy's Bear." And that is how
teddy bears came to be."*

I also told Corey that in the Southwest, among Native Americans, the bear represents the body and healing, and that the bear was present in his body in a powerful way. Corey coughed and sighed. "I know what that wounded bear felt like," he said.

He also knew about power. Corey knew how to "show up for life." He wasn't a quitter. But when the time came and his body had no strength left to go on, this courageous little boy said, "Life is like living in a little apartment... It's not very permanent. Sometimes you just have to move on to a bigger space." Corey died on Independence Day...free at last from an "apartment" that was too small.

The Lesson

Death reminds us of the lesson of impermanence. The body is not permanent. But we are more than our bodies. That lesson is all around us. Energy transcends form. Look at the wind—it cannot be seen but it is real. It can be felt. Love is also an invisible thing. But we feel it. We believe in it. Many who have experienced the loss of loved ones feel their presence in dreams and visions.

Corey knew he would continue on in some form. He had great confidence in that.

Living the Lesson

Death brings up many feelings that need to be acknowledged. Practice this exercise after experiencing a loss.

Breathe. Pay attention to your breath. Let the feelings come up. Feel the feelings in your body. Feel the physical sensation of having feelings. Sadness can feel like a lump and beyond that a burning sensation. Anger can feel like an ache or a stomach in knots. Be uninvolved with the feelings but fully present to the physical experiences of the body.

The feelings are a "what is." This is the moment. Not to be judged, feared, or attended to with attachment. Just observe. Breathe and pay attention.

Like the seasons of nature, all things change and return, come and go.

As you observe, you will begin to see the sensations change. The knots loosen, the burning dissipates. Let it go. Do not cling.

Corey drew bears. What distinguished them were the symbols he drew on the chest. These symbols were to represent the inner, invisible qualities. Try drawing your family members as teddy bears. On the chest draw a symbol for each person in the family. A flame. A thunderbolt. A feather. Talk about these inner, enduring qualities as a family.

now and zen

Chapter 9

*Your old life was a frantic running from
silence. The speechless full moon comes
out now.*

—Rumi

The mind can be like a pot of overcooked soup.
Experiences go into the soup and become
memories. These memories, after bubbling away
for years, become dried out. They no longer
contain a true representation of experience. The
old grudges, the blaming memories, and the
feelings of woundedness, had best be thrown
out like old soup.

By returning often to silence we can begin to
turn off that fire and pour out that overdone
mixture of pain and ego demands, plans and bad
memories. In so doing, we are able to accept
new experiences for what they really are. Often,
it is a hard task to get there. The soup pot is
heavy and the stuff inside sticks to the sides. But
when the turmoil is gone the new clarity of
vision is like the fresh, renewing waters of a
mountain spring. With this clarity, we respond
more freely and fully to life. And we are
prepared for the challenge of helping our
children deal with their fears and tears. We will
find pure peace in the stillness of this emptying.

Zen at the Grocery Store

The mother had a two-year-old daughter in her shopping cart who was trying to open the food her mother had put in the basket. Meanwhile her five-year-old son was racing ahead pointing at the things he wanted to buy. Not realizing that cans must be taken from the top of the stack, he pulled a soup can out of the middle—just as his Mom yelled, "No!" Everyone in the store heard the crash as the entire display of soup cans smashed to the floor. Meanwhile, the two-year-old was working herself up for a tantrum because she wanted to be able to walk around like her brother.

The mother had learned about Zen. She didn't want to explode at her children, so she took a deep breath and closed her eyes. She tuned out the sounds of her daughter and the soup cans rolling down the aisles. She tuned out the people who were staring at her accusingly. She tuned into her own frustration—recognizing it and accepting its presence—and she slowly allowed it to dissipate.

When she opened her eyes again, her daughter was staring at her. The girl had postponed her tantrum to puzzle over what happened to Mom. The son had come quietly back to his mother's side and the store clerk was busily re-doing the display. The other customers were moving on.

Mom decided to change the situation. "Tommy, I'm going to let you and your sister pick out the peaches. I really need your help today," she said. Peace reigned again—at least in this moment!

The Lesson

Does Zen offer easy answers to things such as grocery store tantrums? Or better yet, do the children of Zen parents never have such tantrums? Will children always respond as the previous incident suggests? No, of course not.

What Zen does offer is a tool called mindfulness and an attitude of openness, humor, and flexibility. These tools help alleviate the tensions that arise when our children descend into public displays of craziness! If we can take some time for reflection we know where and when such tantrums are likely to occur. This allows us the opportunity to plan strategies.

If a child tends to throw tantrums right after lunch because she is tired—but won't nap anymore—then it makes sense NOT to go shopping right after lunch. This may be a no-brainer, but we parents sometimes lose sight of the obvious. If the child throws tantrums in the grocery store because she is having a "gimme" attack, then we can find ways to re-direct the child's attention.

Children love to feel they have a job to do and something to contribute. Some stores now have child-sized shopping carts. To bring home bruised or unripe pears picked out by your child is probably preferable to a scream session. And the child who participates in "important work" feels rewarded in a way that is far better than getting something sweet as a result of needling mom.

When children are 10 or 12, we can introduce them slowly to full participation in family shopping. There are many teachable moments about budgets, math, nutrition, and shopping for best quality and not by brand.

So what is "Zen" in all of this? A Zen perspective is a thoughtful perspective. Zen masters are always ready to find the humor and re-direct awareness in any troubling situation. Such skills are learned by taking time for quiet reflection and by putting an end to self-blame and heavy judgments. Every parent makes mistakes and does things incorrectly. The only answer is to "try, try, and try again"—paying ever-closer attention to the lessons from each instance.

Living the Lesson

Parents and children can come up with strategies for coping with difficult situations. Try telling your young children the following story and ask for their ideas about what this Mom can do. Make up as long a list as possible. All answers are acceptable (even crazy ones!).

"A Mom needs to go get the groceries for supper. She takes her son (daughter) with her. But the child doesn't want to ride in the cart and he asks Mom to buy everything they see and he tries to put these things in the cart. Even when Mom says 'no' the child stands in the middle of the aisle complaining about wanting this or that. Mom is very unhappy. What should the mom do?"

If Mom makes the first answer a funny one—such as, "I could ship you to the moon where you can beg and complain all you want"—the children will feel free to see this as a brainstorming game rather than a recrimination for past wrong-doing.

Zen=Natural Laws

Sally liked to sing. She listened to her parents' old tapes and sang the songs to herself at night or when she was alone in her room. But very few people had heard her voice.

One day, on her way home from school, Sally decided to push past her self-conscious fears and sing out loud for all to hear. She went past many closed doors as she sang. Then she saw two older women sitting in chairs outside their houses. When she spotted them she stopped. To sing or not to sing? What would they think? But something inside her said, "Sing." And so she clutched her books more tightly to her chest and started to sing. One of the women smiled and waved. The other one frowned and shook her head. Sally tried not to take it personally. That's what her dad always said—"You never know why people act the way they do. Maybe they were just zapped by a porcupine. So, don't interpret. Just be yourself." She sang all the way home from school, and she enjoyed herself, without caring about what anyone else thought.

The Lesson

Sally did a brave thing—she dared to be herself. When we do as Sally did, we send love out freely into the world, and it returns to us in abundance. It also makes us feel good inside. We have identified five natural laws:

1. What goes around comes around, so if you are a happy, loving person, expect happy, loving people in your life.

2. Doing 'nothing' is something. Either it is positive or negative but it is something. So remember "nothing" is a choice. To sing or not to sing, that is the question.

3. Actions have consequences—there is a cause and an effect.

4. Rhythms give a sense of balance to life. Thus, it is useful to have regular times for waking, eating, playing, and working. Work should be done in a routine way, without struggle. This allows the mind freedom to enjoy the moment.

5. Extremes are the way of society. Balance is a mid-point that society does not achieve. So to be balanced is to live outside the social norms of a political "right" and "left." It is a place of sanity.

To resist these natural laws is foolish because resistance creates struggle and unhappiness. It is best to flow with the things that happen as a part of life. How many people will die? 100%. How many people will experience some failures in life? 100%. How many people will experience loss, rejection, or abandonment? 100%. Life happens. Let it.

Living the Lesson

There is an old song that says, "You gotta sing when the Spirit says 'sing'." So try this. Remember a song from your childhood and sing it. Teach it to your children. Sing it in the car. Find ways to share it with many, because singing—if it is clear and strong and happy—brings happiness to others even if you are off-key. Teach your children to love singing and sharing.

Hospital Zen

*Six-year-old Peter jumped into the air on a trampoline.
He flipped himself over and came down on his thumb.
There was immediate, searing pain. He looked stunned
as he held out his hand. It looked bizarre—his thumb
bent straight back, flattened down towards his wrist. We
rushed off to the Emergency Room. And then we waited,
because that's what you do in emergency rooms.*

*We went into the inner room to wait for a specialist who
would decide what this bizarre thumb required. I worked
with Peter to focus on relaxing since the thumb was no
longer causing pain. I told jokes and encouraged Peter to
think about the day as a grand adventure. By the time
the nurse came in to check on him, Peter was ready to
share his own joke. "We are called 'patients' because we to
have to be 'patient'—right?"*

*Meanwhile, I released my own fears and worries. I
focused on the moment and the fun of being in this
strange place with nothing to do but tell stories. I helped
Peter focus on enjoying the moment. After two hours of
waiting, praying, and joke telling, Peter's thumb
suddenly popped back into place all by itself! The
specialist who came to look at it was quite surprised.
Why had he been called in on a Saturday for nothing?
The nurse assured him it had been "something" just
moments before.*

A small, yet profound miracle had occurred.

114   The Lesson

Miracles happen!

Children believe in the everydayness of miracles. It is adults
who have stopped believing. Is a belief in miracles compatible
with Zen? Certainly. Except in Zen they aren't expected,
anticipated, or requested. They just happen. A Zen practice asks
us to live in the newness of each moment and such is the
perspective necessary for miracles. To see and to experience
opens the door for that childlike perspective that believes
anything can happen. It is when we anticipate and expect—
when we decide ahead of time what can or cannot happen—
that's when we shut out the possibility for miracles.

When Peter waited for the doctor he had no idea what might
happen next. But I knew. The gymnastics teacher told me,
"They will numb the area with a big needle full of pain-killer
and then yank his thumb back into place." So I simply tried to
help Peter enjoy the many moments there in the hospital,
while stilling my own fears. When he was busy working on
jokes, I went into my inner quiet place to meditate. I looked up
a short while later and all was well. His finger popped back
into place because we were both able to relax, to breathe and
let go of anxiety, allowing the body to heal itself and not fight
with the mind.

Yes, miracles do happen.

Living the Lesson

Spend 10 minutes looking into a candle flame. Watch the
movement. See it flicker. Watch the colors…what are they?
Become totally present to the candle. Let the image, the slight
heat, and the delicate crackling become your total experience.

Let yourself experience the miracle of the candle. It is a light in the darkness, helping you to open to greater awareness. Become fully aware of the candle. Do this exercise with your child. Help the child see the candle. Be open to how fully aware your child is of this simple, yet beautiful experience. The stillness of the moment can, and does, create miracles. They are the result of our willingness to let life happen without stress and expectation.

day-to-day
parenting

The best way to stay focused on the beauty and meaning of the present moment is to practice taking regular "time outs." By doing this yourself, you teach your children the beauty and necessity of slowing down, reducing tensions, and appreciating a few moments alone. Take time every day, especially when you feel irritated or distracted, to listen to yourself. Tell your child, "I'm taking a time out." Find a quiet spot and still your mind. When we take time for quiet reflection, we will find the help we need.

Try to do this daily Zen practice:

- ❀ Stay.
- ❀ Stay with the moment.
- ❀ Stay with your attention on your inner awareness.
- ❀ Pay attention. Remember, emotions pass. Bodily needs pass.
- ❀ What stays is the essence of you and the pure spirit of your child.

Take time for quiet reflection many times each day. Every day is a new beginning, with lessons to be learned.

Keeping Promises

*We were on the way to school and my son squirmed in
the back seat of the car, kicking at the back of my seat.
He asked, "Can we go to Jimmy's house after school? It's
been forever since we've been there. Can we go? Can we?
I need to see him. He's my best friend. Please. Please."*

*Then my daughter chimed in, "Yes, yes, yes, yes."
Distracted by the kicking, the pleading, and the
oncoming traffic, I said, "Yes, we can do that today."A
chorus of cheers came from the back seat.*

*Then it hit me. I'd forgotten the discipline I'd been
working on: Don't make promises you can't keep. It is far
better to say, "We'll see." Or, "I'll think about it."After all, a
promise should be kept and never made about
something that may not happen. In this case, I didn't
really think there would be time after school. We had
errands to run and Jimmy was usually involved in after-
school activities. But, I had taken the easy way—say "yes"
now, figure it out later.*

*In those days, I believed I could accomplish more in a
day than was actually possible. Such dreaming left me
exhausted and guilty, while my children were beginning
to show they didn't trust me. That was when I began
to work on the discipline of not promising what I
couldn't deliver.*

*When I picked up the children from school that
afternoon, I hoped and prayed they wouldn't ask, "Are we
going to Jimmy's house?" But of course, that was the first*

thing they asked. And I had to say, "No." My son said, "You never do what you say you're going to do!"

Lesson learned...finally.

The Lesson

While parents often don't notice it, children seek boundaries. They need predictable schedules and people they can count on. There is a sense of safety that comes from boundaries, from knowing what will/can happen today. When children know the outer edges of what is possible they can focus their efforts within that framework. When the limits are open-ended, they are faced with the infinite.

For most children, and adults, as well, infinity is scary (one definition of infinity is chaos). And, even for those who like hanging out on the outer edges of life—it's still part of the human condition to seek limits. For example, the astronaut looked at space, decided to make a space journey to Mars and believed it was possible. The astronaut defined the goal, determined it was within the boundaries of the possible, and set out to reach it. Life always has boundaries. Of course, the ultimate boundaries of existence are birth and death.

Children want to know what is possible. They want to know what boundaries you are setting. They need opportunities. They need new possibilities. But, they also need to know that sometimes things aren't possible. One of the difficult jobs of parenting is to help children understand possibilities, limits, and where/when to trust in the unknown. These are big life lessons.

It is helpful if we can plan ahead so children know what to expect each day. There must be room for flexibility and spontaneity but establishing the limits of the day is one of our

120 responsibilities. Children always want to know, "What can I count on? What can I believe in?"

When we are dishonest with ourselves and/or our children about what is possible, children can easily conclude that the world is unsafe. When children are young they need to know that, yes, there are things we do each day. Sometimes these things change, but mostly there are patterns that can be counted on. Nature's patterns give the emerging flower what is needed. The sun shines, the rain comes, the bugs have their day. And, through it all, the plant usually survives.

Be like nature! If you water a wilting flower in the garden, its life and vibrancy will be renewed. This is a law of science…a reality of life. Such natural laws are what children seek to understand. Children should trust that adults keep their promises. When adults create a life that is too busy to keep their promises, the end result will eventually be an explosion— a need for change. It is like mixing vinegar and baking soda.

Living the Lesson

Try this experiment. Find a small jar (baby-food size). Sprinkle one teaspoon of baking soda into it. Then add in a teaspoon of vinegar. The unexpected happens. It becomes a foamy explosion!! It's fun to see. But in life such explosions are less appealing.

Write in your journal about the importance of keeping promises and developing a rhythm and routine in your family life.

We Are the Role Models

It was time for school and Jerry came out wearing shorts, revealing his long, gangly legs partially covered by one long sock and one short sock.

"If you are going to wear socks, they should match," his mom said.

That's when the whining and complaining began. "I don't have any matching socks. They are all different. And these are both long. See?" (He stopped long enough to pull up the short sock.)

"And I like these just like this. How come I always have to change something? You never like what I pick out. And I want to eat now! And..."

Just then, his younger brother came out of the bathroom and stood with his hands on his skinny hips. Taking a deep breath, he looked at his brother and said, in a voice of calm authority, "I know you have lots of matching socks because Mom just washed them and put them away in your drawer. Better look again, silly." He turned and marched into his room.

The Lesson

It's always a pleasure when a child mimics our behavior during a time when we were calm, reasonable, and at our best. Clearly, the younger brother is reflecting his mom's example. But where did the older boy learn his behavior? Who is he modeling? With the younger boy's favorable image in tow, we can find courage to face the image of the other child to see where he may be learning his quick frustration. What tone of voice do we use when there are many demands?

121

122 Children tend to pull us in many directions. On some days, we know how to handle this with calm authority. But then there are the days when we have our own agenda, our own needs. And the pulling here and there—the demands for food, attention, refereeing of fights and pleas for more things—becomes just too much.

The tension that results can lead to very understandable irritation and frustration. And so we say things such as: "Why do you always argue? Why can't you think before you put your socks on?" Such frustrations are common, but the exaggerations in our speech, such as, "Why do you *always*...?" can lead children to turn life's small challenges into catastrophes. "Why do I *always* have to... You *never* like..."

Still, the good modeling does catch on. The younger brother spoke calmly and in a reasoned, helpful tone. He modeled a behavior that will be helpful later in life. Being self-aware is important. When a child's behavior is irritating, it is a trigger to pay attention and observe how that might be learned from us. In that way, the behavior is a gift. A wake-up call.

As a thousand Zen Masters have challenged: Be here now.

Living the Lesson

Plan to observe your child today.

- ❀ Does he or she become frustrated; does he or she show patience?
- ❀ Does he or she complain; does he or she offer praise?
- ❀ Does he or she argue; does he or she offer compromises?
- ❀ Does he or she say the food is "icky" before trying it; does he or she eat well?

🌸 Does he or she shuffle his or her feet when talking to a neighbor; does he or she respond respectfully to the neighbor?

🌸 Does he or she assume the worst; does he or she believe in what is possible?

Be aware that it is easier to focus on the negative behaviors rather than the positive, helpful attitudes in our children. The "bad" behaviors seem to wear neon signs, while the "good" behaviors wear invisible paint. Usually, both are present. Some days go more smoothly than others. Just be aware—without judgment. And, in the children's behavior take a close look and see if you can see yourself.

You might argue that the words above are "judgments," but honest assessments are not the same as condemning, generalized judgments. If you say, "He complained five times today," that may be honest. But to go from there to say, "He's a chronic complainer. He always complains. He's going to get nowhere in life with his bad attitude," you are making conclusions that get in the way of a good relationship with your child. Such conclusions can set up a child for failure.

Honesty can open the door for reflection and change:

🌸 What can I do to help my child change these behaviors?

🌸 Do I complain? Do I offer praise?

🌸 Do I argue? Do I offer compromises?

🌸 Do I expect the worst? Do I enjoy what is offered today?

🌸 Do I ignore or avoid the people around me? Do I pay attention to others?

🌸 Do I believe in a world of high potential and possibilities?

124   Rewarding the Good

After school there was a carnival/fundraiser in the gym. As the children waited in line for a chance at the ring toss, fishing, and a cakewalk, two brothers began to stand out from the crowd in the noisy gymnasium. One was a high school sophomore who was there to help his five-year-old cousin try to shoot baskets.

The little boy pushed the ball a couple of feet into the air and then looked down in abject failure. One of the brothers said, "Come on, Josh, you can do it. Give it another try." The little one tried again and got the ball farther into the air. He was rewarded with a consolation prize. The other said, "You did really great. Most five-year-olds can't even get it close to the hoop but you really got it up there." They moved on.

The older of the two brothers was a college freshman. He was shepherding an eight-year-old girl through the carnival. The girl wanted to be in the cakewalk. The teen encouraged her to dance to the music. He laughed and joked with all the kids.

When I saw the boys return to their table, I approached the family. The boys went to get food for their young charges. I said, "Your boys are very impressive. It's nice to see teenage boys be so caring and generous to younger children." The parents blossomed with pride. I noticed they shared this praise with their sons.

The Lesson

Whether we acknowledge the good done by other people's children, or our own, or our spouse, it is important to do so.

That helps reinforce it. Good that is recognized has the power to grow.

If you tell children they are "real men and women" when they nurture smaller children, you bring that into more conscious awareness and, thus, it happens more often. Words have power. If you merely tell children they are "good" without basing that observation on anything, it has little meaning to them.

What is innate in children, which needs to be acknowledged, is the presence of God…or a Light, if you will. It is only through action that the world can see and benefit from the Light within us. Our job as parents is to help children find their inner light and let it shine for the betterment of the world. Then their self-esteem will blossom because they are reaching worthwhile goals.

We should teach them some of the universal "goods" they should strive to achieve and embody:

* ❀ Kindness to the young and the old
* ❀ Generosity without strings attached
* ❀ Accountability for one's actions
* ❀ Understanding and listening to others
* ❀ Forgiving those who make mistakes or hurt us

Living the Lesson

Meditate on your breath. See it as a light filling your body and then being sent out. Imagine a clear light coming in. Then send out to the world a rose light of love. Breathe. See the bright light on the incoming breath and then the rose light going out to fill the world. Hold the in-breath for a count of five to be filled. Then exhale the out-breath to a count of five.

Living the Adventure Now

The family was on vacation at a national park. The weather was beautiful. The scenery was majestic. The 10-year-old boy said, "Dad, I wanted to see bears but we only saw a deer and an eagle."

The father said, "Only deer and an eagle? Hmm. I saw that deer grazing so close to us we could almost touch it. And the eagle was flying so low its feet were dragging in the river and we could see its huge wingspan. And the weather has been perfect for sleeping out under the stars."

"Yeah, but…"

"No, there are no 'buts' here," said the dad. "This has been perfect for us at this time in our lives…don't you agree?"

The Lesson

So many times parents or children negate the perfection of the moment. Not that it is perfect, with a capital P, but perfect in that it is right for what is needed now, at this time in life. When we learn to experience and teach that every moment is perfect in its own way—even if it's a small "p"—we bring life to life. Every moment is what it was meant to be—for learning, adventure, and growth.

Living the Lesson

Try to spend the whole day responding to every event with the words, "That's great." Don't be sarcastic or cynical. Evaluate each instance for its greatness. Every moment has a lesson. Listen. Pay attention.

zen psychology

Chapter 11

Here are some points for the development of a Zen psychology of child rearing:

* ✿ Zen sees that the opposite temperaments of our children are, in fact, a fullness to be appreciated. Children who are different from their parents reflect a part of our inner, hidden selves. It is a great learning opportunity to be with a child who reflects an opposite perspective.
* ✿ Children are not adults. The only way to understand children is to pay attention to them as unique beings.
* ✿ The only way to find answers to troubling questions is to pay attention to what is happening, listen to input from the people involved, accept advice for what it is (well-meant help from someone else's life), and tune inside for guidance about your life.
* ✿ Children do not come into life with an awareness of rules or definitions of right and wrong. Instead, they will imitate the example set by adults and

siblings. The words you speak that are incongruent with your actions will be ignored. And this dismissal of what is spoken is not defiance. It is a clarity of perception.

❀ Time heals many things. Everything changes eventually. All emotions pass through us. For many "troubles" all you need to do is respond to the moment and give it time. It will be different eventually—that is guaranteed, unless you hold on to it.

❀ To accept life as it comes without judgment or expectation is an art form. But it can be accomplished through the use of techniques discussed in this book. The reason to work at this way of viewing life is that it frees us from the anguish of wanting things to be different than they are. Life just is. Experiences are neither punishments nor reasons to feel like a victim. Life is.

❀ Beauty and goodness are found only in the immediate moment.

In this chapter we look at how to deal with such dynamics as the pecking order of humans, the learning process for children, and un-cluttering the parenting mind. We also look at how parents can create a cohesive family "mission" in order to focus the family's energy on a meaningful way of living.

Not Taking It Personally

Jane was ready to help her son go to bed. Normally, she read Tony a story but on this night Tony said, "I don't want you. I want Daddy to put me to bed."

Jane felt a bit hurt. She liked the nighttime routine. "Okay," she said and went to get her husband. From the next room, she heard Tony laughing with Dad. And a mere five minutes later, Tony was drifting off to sleep.

"What was that?" she demanded when her husband came out of the bedroom. "It can't take five minutes. It takes half an hour."

She was feeling irritated. Her husband was irritated that she was irritated. "He asked for me. We told some jokes and he kissed me good night. Is that a problem?"

Jane stopped talking. Several nights after her son started the nighttime routine with Daddy, he asked for Mommy.

When she came out of the room as Tony was drifting off to sleep, her husband asked, "What was that about? I thought he wanted me to put him to bed."

Jane realized how she had sounded a few days before. "I guess kids change all the time. We'd better not take his preferences personally or he'll learn fast how to pit us against each other!"

The Lesson

Around age two, children often still cling to Mommy at bedtime. But by the end of this tumultuous year they sometimes prefer Daddy to Mommy. It's not really a choice they are making of one parent over another. It is more about changing needs. As children grow they will look to Mommy for some things and to Daddy for others.

Still, it is hard to be the parent who is left out. Our children do a constant dance through their lives, coming close and then moving away. When they are close it feels good. When they move away, the sting of rejection touches us.

But, as adults we must manage our feelings. To do this means we can acknowledge the hurt/anger/fear/disappointment and remember that such feelings are temporary. To act on them could damage a relationship. We can let them pass away or put them in perspective.

When we feel shut out by the actions of our children, it is our responsibility to remember that "shutting us out" is a part of the growing up experience. Children learn to be self-reliant individuals by taking steps away and then coming back. We need to always be there to reassure them of our love and our willingness to guide them. If we are absorbed with feeling hurt, we cannot respond appropriately.

Don't take the behavior of children personally. It's up to you to guide them, teach them, and set boundaries for them. Eventually they will come back to say, "I love you, Mom. I love you, Dad. You were always there for me."

Living the Lesson

Now imagine your child as a growing vine. You are the fence the vine is growing on. But it goes first in this direction and then in that direction. As a fence you are the boundary and the support for the vine. But you cannot control it fully. Watch the vine growing. See the beauty. Feel your strength and stability. You remain firm. Feel the connection between the two—vine and fence.

Zen and Mind Clutter

An old cartoon shows a woman sitting in the living room nursing her new baby. Meanwhile, her toddler and preschooler are playing. They have toys scattered all over the living room. The dishes are still on the table from lunch. The laundry sits nearby still unfolded. Her daughter has taken off her socks and changed her shorts, leaving the dirty ones on the hallway floor.

Just then her husband comes through the door. In a weak voice, she calls out to him, "Honey, would you please straighten that picture on the wall." In the midst of the clutter and with the help of an understanding husband, she grabs on to a piece of sanity.

The Lesson

Living with small children means living with some amount of clutter most of the time. Toys are dropped here and there; others are placed lovingly on the kitchen counter for mom. Drawings cover the refrigerator and clothes are strewn halfway to the laundry room—never quite reaching their destination! That's the way it is and it's okay.

Most parents are overwhelmed by the chaos young children create and we go through the house on a regular basis cleaning up the mess. Depending on one's ability to handle clutter, such cleanings are hourly, weekly, or monthly. Now, let's be honest, Zen tends toward simplicity and orderliness, even austerity. So, perhaps we must settle for keeping an uncluttered mind in a cluttered house.

After all, the mind is even harder to keep organized and clean. Mind clutter includes all those things we would like to focus on if we ever had the time. When we don't focus on them, but focus on the need to focus on them they end up taking up a lot of mental space. They turn into nagging annoyances that cause us to look for excuses, thinking about when we will focus on them. Mind clutter causes us to leave the *now* where we should be living.

Unlike children's stuff and clutter, mind clutter is much more consuming. Children's clutter can be taken care of at the end of each day but mind-clutter demands a minute-by-minute focus. This is when we need our Zen practice. That time we have set aside to release it all. A time to step away from our mental clutter and move into a feeling of unity with Oneness.

Living the Lesson

Kid clutter and mind clutter can be taken care of in the same way. Here are some thoughts on how to combat both:

- ❀ Sing when things get overwhelming. Focus on the song rather than the clutter. Work to clean up the messes and enlist the children's help, but don't drown in inadequacy if the clutter continues. It is what it is.
- ❀ Meditate to find mind-quiet. Use a mantra—"God is with me, I am with God." Repeat phrases such as this that have merit. They help still the mind clutter. Then it is easier to go about straightening the kid clutter.
- ❀ Learn to laugh and tell jokes. See the humorous side to life.
- ❀ Remember: This too shall pass. Children who are old enough should try picking up after themselves. And by the time they are seven or eight, they should be good at it!

✿ Practice being mindful—one thing at a time. "When I walk, I walk," is an old Zen saying. "When I eat, I eat. When I clean, I clean. When I cook, I cook." Just do what needs to be done in the moment, without judgment or expectation.

The point is not to fill the mind with more "shoulds" but rather to release the mind clutter through a healthy sense of reality.

The Zen Mission

(This story was contributed by Mary Anne Thomas, author of *Ask and You Shall Receive* and *The Power of Creative Prayer*.)

The son complained that his mother had not washed his favorite jeans. He sullenly sat through meals and disappeared quickly. He was hostile when asked questions about where he was going. He was an angry teenager.

His mother, Mary Anne, was a counselor who worked with mothers and families. She gave other people advice, but she had no idea what to do about her own son. One day, she had an insight. She would create a "Good News Board" to focus on the positives in the life of her family. Even if no one else joined in, the "Good News" would help her focus on the things that went well rather than filling her mind with worries.

Mary Anne put the dry-erase board up the next day, and called a family meeting to discuss its use. She explained, "It's a place to list all the good news that happens to everyone in our family. Wait til you see what happens!" she coached. "You'll really feel good. You'll feel supported and encouraged. Everyone can use more support, right?" Silence greeted her.

Then the son interrupted to ask, "Is the meeting over yet? I've got friends waiting outside." She nodded quietly.

Each day, Mary Anne listed a few items on her family's "Good News Board," such as, "We got that $93 refund I requested from VISA today," "Anne got an A on the science test she was worried about," "Colin washed off the back deck and I was able to enjoy my morning tea outside today."

No one else wrote on the board at first, but on the fourth day, her daughter Anne wrote something. Soon, the others added items—personal items concerning school events and relationship changes.

A week later, Mary Anne sensed a new atmosphere in the house. There were more smiles, fewer conflicts. But her angry son was the last to climb on the Good News wagon. A month after it began, he wrote his first note. And one day he came home from school, wrapped his arms around Mary Anne and said, "I'm sorry I was so rough on you for a while there, Mom. I guess I was going through something."

Mary Anne's Good News Board helped her teenager begin to notice some of the good things going on around him. It gave the family a mission—to be positive and find gratitude daily. She said, "It softened our hearts."

Just a few short years after this mission of making daily gratitude a part of their family life, Mary Anne's son was killed in a car accident.

She explained, "I'm so glad I had a chance to see him break out of that sullen phase. Otherwise, I might not have known how he really felt about me. I might have remembered his angry, bullying complaints and wondered whether he had ever loved me. But now, I have the memory of his arms wrapped around me, and I can hear his softly apologetic words ringing in my ears, and I know for sure that he loved and appreciated me."

The Lesson

Mary Anne's technique helped the members of her family focus on the family's daily experiences—things that would otherwise have passed unnoticed. For the teenage son who was experiencing hormonal surges and peer pressures, it helped him become more grounded in the life of the family.

A similar technique is one we have used in businesses and in families. The idea is that we need a focus for the family (or business). It helps solidify the identity of the whole and gives inspiration for how to live. The following is a business "mission statement"* that could be easily be used for family life.

(*Personal Mission for Keers Industries' Co-Workers, Albuquerque, NM, courtesy of Brian Kilcup, CEO)

136   Every Day Brings New Challenges, Therefore:

     ✿ We Accept Them
     ✿ We Overcome Them
     ✿ We Learn and Persist

We're teaching this mission to our children, as well. It is an excellent reminder to accept "what is" without judgment and to do our best with it.

A mission statement and a Good News Board can be commitments to daily practice.

Living the Lesson

Plan a family meeting to discuss the Mission Statement for your family. Talk about the things that are important to you. Consider such things as: gratitude, adventure, service, integrity— honoring our commitments, trustworthiness, acceptance of differences, loving kindness to all, and achievement.

Post your Mission Statement in a prominent place and use a Dry-Erase board to allow family members to write down how they have implemented the mission each day. Make it a family time to discuss the mission statement and how it has affected the identity of your family.

Football Zen

*They were in the hotel pool when I met them. Freddie
was about nine years old. His mother was trying to teach
him to throw a football. "Please Freddie. This can be fun,
really," she pleaded.
When Freddie missed the ball and turned away, his
mother jumped up on to the edge of the pool and
whispered to me, "His father is always critical of him.
Freddie thinks he'll never be able to do any sports. I just
want him to try."*

*Mom jumped back in the pool and went closer to her
son. She coaxed, "Freddie, let's just have fun. There isn't
any way to learn to throw the ball other than to practice.
Just hold your fingers on the seam and give it a toss.
Trust yourself. It'll come naturally after a while."*

*But Freddie still refused to try. He took the ball and threw
it about 10 feet without paying any attention to where
he was throwing it. His mother was dedicated to her task.
She elicited my help. "Ma'am," she called to me, "Would
you like to catch?" She tossed the ball in my direction. I
jumped up in the water and was surprised when my
hands actually managed to hold on to the ball!*

*"Wow," I shouted. "I caught it!" The mom laughed as she
saw my enthusiasm. "It's fun when you can do it...but it
doesn't happen all the time. Try throwing it. You know—
put your fingertips on the seam and keep your eyes on
me. Then let the ball kind of roll off your fingertips."*

*I had never learned to throw a football but I was happy
to help out. I positioned my fingers on the ball, pulled my*

arm back and looked at the other woman across the pool and threw it. Out of the corner of my eye, I saw Freddie had an intrigued look on his face. My throw fell about two feet short of the woman and splashed her with a big spray. She wiped her face and laughed. "Good throw," she said, "I should have caught that." We threw the ball to each other several times. I was pleased that my throws were getting better and I was actually catching the ball. We were basically ignoring Freddie. But he was trying to get our attention.

"Throw it here, okay?" he called. We began a three-way game. Gently, Freddie's mom gave instructions between laughter and splashes. She encouraged her two students to make eye contact and concentrate on where we wanted the ball to go. Freddie was getting better. "Great spin, Freddie. You have a good arm," she called.

After half an hour of throwing, my arm was aching. We took a break. Freddie's mother sat near me in the spa. She whispered, "You know what? I have never thrown a football before today! But I've seen my husband do it."

She was amazing. I never did learn her name—but a few hours later I saw Freddie throwing a football to his younger sister. He was now the authority—confident that he could both throw and catch. His mother saw me leaving and called out, "Mission accomplished."

The Lesson

Learning to throw a football is a bit like learning to raise a child. If we think too much about it, our mind gets in the way! And if it seems like work or that someone will judge us for not always being on target, we will sabotage our efforts.

To learn to throw you keep your mind on the target—in parenting, we do the same. The goal is to be the best parent we can be so our children will unfold as they need to. The more we focus and practice listening for that inner guidance, the better we will get at it.

Teaching children to be confident and capable in life requires that parents demonstrate their own confidence and capability. There is a story about how Benjamin Franklin got the people of colonial Pennsylvania to adopt the use of streetlights. He didn't beg and plead at town meetings. He didn't put up flyers endorsing the virtues of his new idea. He didn't argue with those who would be critical. He merely hung a lantern in front of his house. Each night he lit the lantern. The townspeople appreciated the glow from his light as they passed by his house at night. Soon a neighbor asked Mr. Franklin to help him set up a lantern. And in a short time everyone was doing it.

The willingness of one person to try something new can set the example for a whole town. Children learn best when they see those they love being willing to learn new skills. Children learn by example. So be strong and admit when you don't know the answers. Be generous and be willing to accept help. Be forgiving of those who have wronged you, but stand up to those who would continue to wrong others. Try to be a model of behavior worthy of your child.

Living the Lesson

Throw a football with your children. Feel the grip of your fingers on the seam. Point the ball where you want it to go. Pull back your arm. Bring it forward and let the ball roll off your fingers. See your hand following through; your arm extended to the point where the ball is to go.

Throwing a ball is very Zen. It is an "in the moment" experience. And the more you focus on the feel of the ball and the direction you want it to go—while releasing self-judgments, memories of when the throw didn't work, and your fears that you aren't good enough—the better you will be able to accomplish the task.

And this is what we do as parents: We experience the moment. We give the children the guidance (and boundaries) they need. And when they are ready, we send them on their way to become who they are meant to be.

Bibliography

Zen Books

These readable books provide a good introduction to Zen wisdom.

Chodron, P. 2002. *The Places That Scare You: A Guide to Fearlessness in Difficult Times.* Boston, MA: Shambhala.

Fischer, N. 2003. *Taking Our Places: The Buddhist Path to Truly Growing Up.* San Francisco, CA: Harper San Francisco.

Gunaratana, V.H. 1994. *Mindfulness in Plain English.* Boston, MA: Wisdom Publications.

Herrigel, E. 1999. *Zen in the Art of Archery.* New York: Random House.

Katagiri, D. 1988. *Returning to Silence: Zen Practice in Daily Life.* Boston, MA: Shambhala.

Kornfield, J. 1993. *A Path With Heart: A Guide Through the Perils and Promises of Spiritual Life.* New York: Bantam Books.

Reps, P. & N. Senzaki 1994. *Zen Flesh, Zen Bones.* Boston, MA: Shambhala.

Rinpoche, S. 1994. *The Tibetan Book of Living and Dying.* San Francisco, CA: Harper San Francisco.

Shoshanna, B. 2002. *Zen Miracles: Finding Peace in an Insane World.* New York: John Wiley & Sons, Inc.

142   Suzuki, S. 1986. *Zen Mind, Beginner's Mind*. New York: Weatherhill, Inc.

Tart, C. 1994. *Living the Mindful Life*. Boston, MA: Shambhala.

Trungpa, C. 1988. *The Myth of Freedom*. Boston, MA: Shambhala.

Parenting Books

The following books are by authors we have interviewed or worked with in the creation of our magazine *Parenting With Spirit*. Each of these works is inspiring and practical.

Biro, B. 2000. *Through the Eyes of the Coach: The New Vision for Parenting: Leading, Loving and Living*. Asheville, NC: Pygmalion Press.

Brooks, R. & S. Goldstein 2001. *Raising Resilient Children*. Chicago, IL: Contemporary Books.

Dancy, R.B. 2000. *You Are Your Child's First Teacher*. Berkeley, CA: Celestial Arts.

Kabat-Zinn, M. & J. Kabat-Zinn. 1997. *Everyday Blessings: The Inner Work of Mindful Parenting*. New York: Hyperion.

Kaplan, J. & A. Lederman 2002. *Finding the Path: A Novel for Parents of Teenagers*. Wyncote, PA: Hawk Mountain Press.

Kurcinka, M.S. 1998. *Raising Your Spirited Child Workbook*. New York: HarperCollins.

Reichlin, G. 2001. *The Pocket Parent*. New York: Workman Publishing.

Seligman, M. 1995. *The Optimistic Child*. Boston, MA: Houghton Mifflin Co.

Spangler, D. 1998. *Parent as Mystic, Mystic as Parent*. New York: Riverhead Books.

Related Books
On divorce:
Wittmann, J. 2001. *Custody Chaos, Personal Peace: Sharing Custody With an Ex Who's Driving You Crazy*. New York: Perigee.

On death:
Housden, M. 2002. *Hannah's Gift: Lessons From a Life Fully Lived*. New York: Bantam.

On life as a celebration:
Thomas, M.A. 2002. *The Power of Creative Prayer*. Long Beach, CA: RICH University.

On offering service and compassion to the world:
Le Joly, E. & J. Chaliha 2000. *Reaching Out in Love: Stories Told by Mother Teresa*. New York: Continuum.

144   Other Resources

The Blue Mountain Center of Meditation offers workshops and books on meditation practices as taught by Eknath Easwaran. Box 256, Tomales, CA 94971, 800-475-2369. www.nilgiri.org

Edward deBono's writings are excellent for teaching creative and lateral thinking to children. He also writes about humor and its importance in teaching children to explore multiple answers for every given problem. His website is www.edwdebono.com.

A good place to go for help in understanding and addressing the needs of a child who has learning and/or behavioral challenges is the website www.SchwabLearning.org.

Music for children:
Bill Harley, "Down in the Backpack" (www.billharley.com)

Danae Shanti, "Lullabies for Little Visionaries," produced by Sounding Free Music, 2000.

Any classical music